YEAH, NAH!

Also by William McInnes

A Man's Got to Have a Hobby

Cricket Kings

The Making of Modern Australia

(with Essential Media & Entertainment)

That'd Be Right

Worse Things Happen at Sea (with Sarah Watt)

The Laughing Clowns

The Birdwatcher

Holidays

Full Bore

Fatherhood

Christmas Tales

WILLIAM McINNES

YEAH, NAH!

A CELEBRATION OF LIFE AND THE WORDS THAT MAKE US WHO WE ARE

hachette
AUSTRALIA

These are my memories. The names and descriptions of some people have been changed so that they too can preserve their own memories, in their own ways.

William McInnes

hachette
AUSTRALIA

Published in Australia and New Zealand in 2023
by Hachette Australia
(an imprint of Hachette Australia Pty Limited)
Gadigal Country, Level 17, 207 Kent Street, Sydney, NSW 2000
www.hachette.com.au

Hachette Australia acknowledges and pays our respects to the past, present and future Traditional Owners and Custodians of Country throughout Australia and recognises the continuation of cultural, spiritual and educational practices of Aboriginal and Torres Strait Islander peoples. Our head office is located on the lands of the Gadigal people of the Eora Nation.

Copyright © William McInnes 2023

This book is copyright. Apart from any fair dealing for the purposes of private study, research, criticism or review permitted under the *Copyright Act 1968*, no part may be stored or reproduced by any process without prior written permission. Enquiries should be made to the publisher.

A catalogue record for this book is available from the National Library of Australia

ISBN: 978 0 7336 5065 9 (paperback)

Cover design by Christabella Designs
Cover photograph courtesy of Getty Images
Author photo by Claudia Scalzi
Typeset in 12.7/19.2 pt Bembo Std by Bookhouse, Sydney
Printed and bound in Australia by McPherson's Printing Group

The paper this book is printed on is certified against the Forest Stewardship Council® Standards. McPherson's Printing Group holds FSC® chain of custody certification SA-COC-005379. FSC® promotes environmentally responsible, socially beneficial and economically viable management of the world's forests.

Dedicated to everyone who has helped create the Australian language

CONTENTS

Introduction 1

1 Simpler times 5
2 Unprecedented times 20
3 Testing times 45
4 A stitch in time 67
5 Sporting times 96
6 The big time 124
7 Changing times 155
8 Wasting time 179
9 Men of their time 206
10 Business time 236
11 Calling time 255

Acknowledgements 279

INTRODUCTION

Yeah, nah.

I love that phrase.

If people want to laugh about the way Australians communicate, one of the first phrases or expressions they usually point to is 'Yeah, nah'.

It might seem gormless but it's actually a phrase of truncated egalitarianism that floats from the lips of Australians in the twenty-first century. From cricketers called Travis who've just hit a ton in a session, from swimmers called Ariarne or Emma who've just won gold or broken a record, to kids in the playground and workers in the office, from people like you and me, and all the rest in between.

It's a succinct distillation of politeness and humility, even if it's just bunged on – and isn't that most of what politeness is? An act to grease the wheels of human communication?

You accept the initial question, the point of view that has been made, and then deflect praise, or politely disagree and offer the chance for further debate on the subject.

Yeah, nah. Maybe it's sloppy grammar and lazy slang dressed up to give it more complexity and weight than it deserves?

Yeah, nah. It deserves appreciation, and a celebration. Come to think of it, so do lots of words and phrases we use to colour the way we communicate.

The way we use language, and the way it is communicated, makes me love being human. Being Australian. We may not, as a species and as a nationality, always be very admirable or at our best, but there are moments of gold that we spin, as we try to reach out to each other. Sometimes we stumble upon such gold and sometimes it is born out of a delight we discover in communicating. Perhaps our expressions indicate the sort of people we are and the souls that we carry within us, for I know the memory of my parents, and the words they used and how they used them to communicate, make me love them even more.

This book isn't just a collection of terms and accompanying definitions, and it's not a catalogue of every piece of slang or vernacular that has ever been uttered in Australia. It is a collection of stories, memories and moments inspired by

INTRODUCTION

Australian language. A celebration of lives and words. And above all, the delight in how we Australians communicate before we drop off our perch.

A man can only live when he lives, and thankfully we live in a time when we can glory in how we construct language and communicate. And we can remember words from other lives that can inform our own times.

Or am I bunging it on a bit too much?

Yeah . . . nah.

CHAPTER 1
SIMPLER TIMES

Round the corner from where I live is a general store that sits just above the beach.

Well, it was once a general store, a last-stop shop for residents of a little village by the bay, where'd they go for things one might need in a pinch, things you may have forgotten, things for brekkie, lunch or dinner. Milk and the papers, soap and washing powder, lollies, ice-cream and soft drink. A modest little pantry for a modest little village.

These days it doesn't pretend to be that anymore. It's like a lot of the other old general stores dotted along the coast. They've become a weekend newspaper magazine's idea of a general store.

There's a shell of the old idea, but instead of a collection of necessities now there are collections of fine wines from top-end local wineries and organic smallgoods at airport prices. There's a collection of jewellery, fancy homewares and ornate things to stick in your garden, also at airport prices.

The general stores and their airport prices. Airport prices are the inflated costs people pay for items at airports for no good reason other than that airports charge higher prices because they can. There are reasons for this phenomenon that people who specialise in marketing will give you – things cost more at airports because rents for the shops and retail areas are higher, because the store holders pay commissions to the airports and pass costs on.

There is also a captive market at airports just waiting to be milked.

And that's exactly what the newspaper magazine's general stores do too: charge more to their usually accepting clientele. So, wherever you might find yourself, when you pay more for items for no identifiable reason you are paying 'airport prices'.

But the general store round the corner from where I live is the nicest and most welcoming one I've been to. It has a very good café, which makes very nice coffee, run by very lovely people. It's no general store, but it keeps the name because people like to be reminded of a time when things were a bit simpler.

Next door to the old general store is a small post office.

It is most definitely a post office, run with welcome efficiency and politeness by a couple who took over from a pair of siblings who, in my mother's terms, 'weren't quite right' for the job. On the rare occasions you managed to receive any mail, you'd be forced to stand at the counter while one of the siblings pointed the barcode scanner at you and proclaimed, 'Wait please, you are now being processed!'

It was even more awkward when they knew what it was that was in the mail. I purchased a crate of lovely pinot noir and went down to collect the wine and was met with a room full of customers waiting patiently to collect their parcels.

'Oh! More wine, William? Is it time to admit that someone might have a problem?'

I was taken aback but a few other people laughed so I thought it was all in good spirits.

Then a week later I was sent a beautiful white rum as a gift, which elicited the following: 'Moving on to spirits? The hard stuff. Cuban white rum!'

I replied that if this brand of rum was good enough for Ernest Hemingway, then it was good enough for William McInnes.

I got a blank look and then the pronouncement that I was entering my 'Relatively Oldish Man and the Sea' period. Or perhaps 'The Largish, Oldish Man and the Sea'. It was good fun.

The post office and the general store are housed in one building and they share a deck. You can loll about with a coffee, chatting to people you've bumped into. Or you can browse at a free lending library on a small table next to a shelf that's home to various in-season citrus fruit that are free to take if you feel the urge.

Standing there, you can look out over the trees and see the bay. A rocky outcrop on the horizon is known as the Nobbies.

One arvo not long ago I stood with my mate Leo and looked out at the bay and the Nobbies. I couldn't help but think of a couple of our friends who had to be rescued from the Nobbies in the 1990s because the inflatable boat they had decided to go sightseeing for seals in was sinking and they were surrounded by sharks.

I reminded Leo of the incident and we laughed a little.

'Jacques Cousteau eat your heart out, you lovely old frog,' Leo said as he sipped his coffee.

The sharks, large ones apparently, were keen for more than just a spot of sightseeing for seals. They were after a seal meal and had mistaken one side of the Zodiac inflatable as lunch and taken a bite. 'The Noahs', as one of my pals onboard described the sharks, then let go of the Zodiac and proceeded to prowl around as their snack began to sink. Thankfully, one of the people onboard was another friend of ours, Phil. Though no Jacques Cousteau, Phil proved more than useful as a bayside Bear Grylls.

Phil was a landscaper who dreamed of coming up with the perfect dirt product: a mixture of shell grit, river soil and, according to Leo, a collection of eleven herbs and spices, or some such stuff. The Colonel Sanders of soil was also the one who had talked my pals into going on the Zodiac inflatable for some seal-spotting. As the Nobbies is a feeding ground for large fish who are quite fond of eating reasonably large sea-going mammals, this didn't really seem the wisest of decisions.

Colonel Sanders redeemed himself though, and went a long way to proving his adventurer status by navigating the sinking Zodiac to a rock where my pals clambered to safety, after nightmarishly stepping on the top of a Noah briefly, which then shied away after the Colonel heftily punched the shark a couple of times.

While we sipped our coffees, Leo added that Phil gave up his dream of being the Colonel Sanders of soil and became a survivalist on Bribie Island in Tasmania.

'Bribie? Is there a Bribie Island in Tasmania?' I questioned. 'I know there's one in Queensland. It's where Max Bygraves died.'

I suddenly thought of my mother.

This only took an instant and memories cascaded down the years and tumbled together to form a portrait in my mind.

In her later years, Mum would go on day trips from the Redcliffe Peninsula, where she still lived in the home my siblings and I grew up in. She'd go with her great chum Mrs Kendall, often venturing to the mythical Twin Towns Club, just across the Queensland border in New South Wales. Twin Towns was the first dip of your toe into the sea of sin and fun away from Queensland: the home of pokies that for so long were banned in the Sunshine State. It also had a galaxy of food stalls, eateries and boutiques, or 'booze-tiques' as my mum called them, because you'd have to be full as a tick to buy anything in them. Airport prices, even back then.

There was also a large cabaret hall where 'international acts' performed. The plan was for the two intrepid daytrippers to set off to see Andy Williams, one of my mum's favourite crooners.

'Oh, lovely voice, nice hair but those teeth! So big, so many, very Dutch-looking, you know, but a lovely voice,' was my mum's neat piece of profiling on Andy 'Dutch' Williams.

After that particular trip, I rang and asked her how it had gone and what 'Dutch' Williams was like.

A scoffing retort boomed down the phone. 'Blow Andy bloody Williams. Couldn't get in to see the Dutch bugger. He was booked out. But I wasn't told. I went along for "Moon River" and got the double bill from hell. It was like expecting to go to the gallops and sit in the stand and you end up at the dish-lickers eating cold pies in the outer.'

'What was the double bill?' I asked.

'Bloody Pam Ayres and Max Bygraves.'

It makes me laugh still.

Max Bygraves was an old Pommy entertainer, a song and dance man. Bit of a song, bit of patter, jokes a bit off maybe, but a man of his time. A reassuring, familiar face who sang singalong songs with sweet melodies and familiar words to those who grew up with him.

He'd ended up getting dementia and moved out to live with his son and family on Bribie Island, so Mum told me.

Some time later, my mum told me down the phone that Max had fallen off the perch. 'Dear old Max. Old Timers got him, but he was with people who loved him, and Bribie is one of the nicer of God's waiting rooms.' My mum had paused and then sounded like she was talking about an old friend. 'He was actually very good that afternoon at Twin Towns, he looked like he enjoyed himself. And we sang along.' Another pause and then, 'Well, as long as he was with people he loved and who loved him. A man can only live when he lives. That's the main thing.'

I knew that my mum was thinking about my old man. He'd had Alzheimer's disease at the end of a colourful and more than useful life. One arvo, out of the blue, my parents had said they wanted to talk to me for they had News. News with a capital 'N', my mum had said.

I must have had a certain look on my face because my mother had then said quickly, 'Oh don't worry, it's not about you, you stupid boy.' She often called me 'stupid boy', even though I was nearly twenty-four by then.

She turned to my dad. 'You have News, don't you, Colin?'

I waited.

My father half smiled and patted the dog.

'Colin?' my mum repeated quietly.

'Yes. News. Oh, I've a touch of the Old Timers disease.'

And he patted the dog again. Alzheimer's disease.

After Mum had told me about Old Max dying on Bribie, she began singing down the phone. She sang for me and

Max and my dad, and maybe for herself. It was an old Max Bygraves song, 'Tiny Bubbles'. An old song from long, long ago, about champagne bubbles and being in love with a big golden moon above, and feeling how you are going to love someone until the end of time.

All this I remembered in a blink and then I heard Leo speaking next to me on the deck.

He'd thought about the island. 'Bribie, yeah, nah. It's the one that sounds like Bribie.' He laughed. 'The Brown-eye island!' By which he meant Bruny Island.

'Yeah, nah,' he said again. 'A survivalist on Brown-eye Island. Now that's a reality show I'd watch!'

We shared another laugh.

Then we both noticed a kid waiting to go into the little post office. She was holding a basket in which sat a large black and white pet rabbit. I assumed it was a pet because there was a large spotted bow around its neck.

'A bloody Tommy Austin!' I muttered.

Where I live there are many, many rabbits. And only a small percentage are pets, the rest are the wretched grey descendants of Tommy Austin, the Pommy colonist who decided to let these pests loose on the Australian landscape back when this continent was being run by people from England who barely knew their arse from their elbow, and almost nothing about the wonderful land that they had claimed as their own.

Whenever I see a rabbit, I recall how my old rugby coach would refer to them as 'Tommy Austins'. He would use this expression when he generously likened us to rabbits. 'You're playing like a pack of Tommy Austins, bloody rabbits, running away when you should be running towards the ball, and all with your heads up your arses – get out there and do something. Anything.'

Tommy Austin, or Thomas Austin to give him his full due, was a pastoralist and member of the Acclimatisation Society of Victoria, a group who wanted to make this part of the world a little more like the Mother Country that they had all left behind.

Down in Geelong in 1859 Tommy thought rabbits might be fair game for a bit of sport shooting and so he released twenty-four breeding rabbits. The rest, as they say, is history.

All that environmental damage and degradation caused by a bloke who missed home. Well, he wouldn't be the last person to try to make another place feel like home and wreak havoc.

I can imagine that coming to Australia in 1859 from England might well have been like arriving on Mars. It's quite human to feel a little frightened and alone, and long for something from home.

But was the answer to this really a rabbit? No.

And now there before Leo and me was living proof of the consequences of homesickness – a bloody Tommy Austin.

I thought maybe the girl might have been taken aback by the tone I'd used, so I attempted to put my rugby coach's view of rabbits aside and be pleasant.

'Taking your rabbit for a picnic?' I asked.

The kid looked at me like I was an idiot.

An older man who was with her said, 'This rabbit would make a good picnic.'

The kid looked at him like he was an idiot too.

'We've just come back from a photo shoot and Pop wanted to check the post.'

'A photo shoot?' said Leo.

'Yes,' the girl said, as if a photo shoot was the most normal thing you would do with a great swollen black and white Tommy Austin in a basket. 'For the school newsletter's pet of the month.' It might have been a *Vogue* front cover, the way she said it.

Her pop laughed and patted her on the back.

'What's your rabbit called?' I asked.

Before she could answer, her pop weighed in. 'Stew,' he said. 'Stew the rabbit, both a name and a statement of intent. That's why he'd make a good picnic.'

The kid took a big breath and said, 'Yeah . . . nah, Poppy.'

Poppy, Leo and I all laughed.

'His name is Buttons,' she said. 'Stew is such a lame joke, Poppy.'

Poppy patted her again. 'Perhaps, but we can only dream.' And they walked into the small post office.

Leo and I wandered off with our coffees and I thought, not for the first time, how the Australian language astounds, confounds and entertains.

'Yeah . . . nah,' the kid had said. 'Yeah, nah,' my mate Leo had said.

I'd heard that phrase just the previous Friday night after a football game on the telly had finished. It's almost a given in any post-match interview. This time it was a National Rugby League player, seemingly genetically built to mirror a Soviet-era concrete worker's statue, although in place of a hammer or sickle and a rolled-up shirt sleeve, they have an arm sleeve of tatts and a mouthguard clenched in their fist. Fresh from the field and professionally prepared to answer the same questions every week, like a traditional litany in some vague ritual of today's communal celebration of belief: a sports broadcast.

An off-camera disembodied voice asks, 'You dominated out there tonight from your first run, was that part of the execution of the game plan?'

The worker's statue, chest heaving in a striped jersey bedecked with the medals of sponsorship, gives the response expected but in a voice that invariably and quite alarmingly sounds softer and much younger than what is expected from a human so big.

'Yeah, nah. Just happy to play well against a quality opposition. Stuck to the basics and happy to contribute. Happy with the win.'

Yeah, nah.

The kid had said it to her grandfather with equal parts love and attitude, and I thought what a lovely human she'd grow up to be.

The words I'd heard around me on that trip to the weekend newspaper magazine's idea of a general store, and my recollections, had bombarded me with colour and delight.

We Australians also love a nickname or diminutive. The Nobbies have the formal geographical title of 'Point Grant on Phillip Island', named after a surveyor and naval officer, Lieutenant James Grant of His Majesty's English naval forces. Grant had quite a meritorious career roaming the globe at His Majesty's behest, mapping, fighting, working in Imperial administration and surveying. He was, by all accounts, a thoroughly decent bloke. 'As a man, he was upright and sincere with a mind of his own as well as being a gallant and skilful officer' is how the *Australian Dictionary of Biography* sums him up.

It sounds like a character description of a Colin Firth type lead, no doubt dressed fetchingly in ruffles and tunic with a suitably pouty expression on his handsome face. The kind who appears in a Sunday evening BBC historical period drama popular in some of the finer Australian suburbs.

In rounded tones he'd soulfully say, 'I survey at His Majesty's grace,' and fetchingly flare his nostrils just for good measure.

Yet, even with all this Firthian nobility of service and character, Point Grant became known as the Nobbies, because of the curious knob-shaped rocks found in the shallows. So the name is based on what people thought the geographical formations looked like instead of what some official proclaimed they should be called. It represents that comfortably rebellious trait of Australians.

Australians also love something a bit more informal. The Nobbies is a bit more familiar and warm than Point Grant and even hints at the promise of a bit of fun. Actually, Nobbies Grant sounds like a character name from some geezer caper film about Cockney lads. ''Ere, check out dis mass of wa'ta wiv dese funny rocks init! Bloody marv-louse, ave this lot sir-veyed in a wink of me eye.' There might have even been a part for old Max Bygraves, or at the least one of his familiar old tunes on the soundtrack.

It's as if those rocks are just a collection of someone's old mates, The Nobbies. Or maybe an English pop band popular in the 1960s who are now on a club and RSL tour of Australia playing all their old hits: 'Live hits of The Nobbies'.

We delight in mangling words and names, rummaging around in our minds to somehow turn Bruny Island into Brown-eye Island – a simple, though perhaps juvenile, piece of fun.

Calling sharks 'Noahs' is old Australian rhyming slang – shark equals Noah's Ark and because we are Australian and shorten everything, Noah's Ark became Noahs, again offering that ring of familiarity and the faint hint of absurdity at the proprietorial nature of Noah and his sharks.

My mother's expression of disappointment when she didn't see Dutch Williams and his brigade of large white teeth and lovely voice, but instead had to sit through Pam Ayres and dear old Max Bygraves, is pure Australian vernacular. Dutch was a top-shelf act, a real treat, and so was akin to sitting in the grandstand at the gallops, that is the horse races, watching thoroughbreds with the other toffs while drinking fizz, champagne. The pinnacle of a day out at the races.

It turned out she didn't get the gallopers but instead Max and Pam, who were akin to eating cold pies at the dish-lickers, otherwise known as the greyhound dog races, a more down-at-heel form of racing entertainment.

Incidentally, greyhounds were a favourite source of metaphor for my father. The nearest dish-licker – sorry, greyhound – track to us in Redcliffe was at Lawnton and this lent itself to a rather lovely expression of my father's to describe beckoning disappointment.

When my father heard my brother had taken a girl out to a Pizza Hut restaurant on a romantic first date and had then wondered why love didn't blossom, he had opined, 'Jesus Christ alive, son, you promised her the world and all you delivered was the Lawnton Dogs! No wonder she's not coming back for another dip.'

The dish-lickers also made an appearance when he was expressing doubt about the Labor Party's prospects in a coming state election: 'We've got about as much a chance to win this as a three-legged greyhound with an eye patch.'

Mum described Bribie Island, where Max Bygraves shared his last days with people he loved and who loved him, as one of God's nicer waiting rooms. A humorous, gentle and reassuring way of putting in perspective what waits for us all.

And of course Max didn't simply die but 'fell off the perch', the way a budgie in a cage might when it dies.

My father's play on words in describing the news that he had to share, as he sat with people he loved and who loved him, that he had 'a touch of the Old Timers' are the words of quiet courage and generosity of an extraordinary ordinary bloke.

It was the beginning of the horrible disease that descended and overwhelmed him, but Alzheimer's was put into a perspective that was manageable. It was something that wasn't to be worried about too much, just a touch of something, perhaps fate or bad luck, that you had to take on the chin and accept.

Maybe it was because my dad and mum's generation were people who didn't think that anything was owed to them, especially by life. They lived and worked and took what came their way, sometimes bending life a little to their own advantage but mostly just dealing with things like most others did. There was no sense of entitlement, no sense that anything was owed to them because of who they were. It was, quite frankly, a rather heroic way of being. Or as some people might like to say, trying to explain a rather selfless view of life, it was simpler times.

CHAPTER 2
UNPRECEDENTED TIMES

When I was very young, and even as I grew older, my mother had a phrase she would utter to all her children, her grandchildren and perhaps even herself, sometimes as a warning or sometimes as a kindly effort to cajole someone out of an impending mood or sulky sook. 'Come on, no Hanrahans here in this family. We're a glass half full mob, so get yourself on the William Jolly Bridge.'

It meant basically to stop moaning, get a grip and get to a happy place where you could deal with the rest of the day.

It may seem a bit of a mouthful but it makes perfect sense to me. A 'Hanrahan' comes from the title character of an old Australian bush ballad, 'Said Hanrahan'. It was written by a priest called Patrick Hartigan, under the pen name John O'Brien, and was in part a quiet homily and a gentle satire on the types of people he found in his parish.

It was read by teachers at school, then recited unsteadily by we students with a decided lack of enthusiasm, for it was hard to get your mouth around how some parts of the poem were written.

This was because, according to our teacher Miss Law, the poem was written in a 'dialect of the bush', which prompted one boy called Russell to attempt a spot of classroom humour by reciting it in a wavery voice, complete with his thumb and forefinger pinching his Adam's apple. He then proceeded to rather violently wobble his throat while interspersing the poem's lines with exclamations of 'Exterminate, exterminate!'

When the teacher asked what he was doing, he stated he was being a 'Dalek from the bush, you know, like from *Dr Who*.'

Russell was given short shrift from Miss Law, who described him as a ning-nong, an irresponsible student, and sent him off to the office for caning.

Miss Law had certain form with her ideas of responsible student behaviour. In February of 1972, not long after we had started to come to terms with the Dalek/dialects of the Australian bush, our classroom television sets were tuned to the ABC for the historic meeting of President Richard Nixon of the United States and Mao Zedong, the Chairman of the People's Republic of China, after decades of barely contained Cold War belligerence.

Not long after the class had begun for the day, we were informed by Miss Law that these two men – the Chinese man in a shapeless grey jacket with a haphazard military cut and the jowly American with dark shiny wavy hair, who looked like he was from the tribe of men who'd flog used cars or washing machines on the television commercials before the Sunday arvo footy replays – had the power to blow up the world in the time it took we students to have 'little lunch'.

Little lunch was morning recess, and big lunch was the day's lunch break.

'You should pray,' Miss Law suggested, 'that we make it through to big lunch . . .' she paused, and ended on a rather chilling note, 'and beyond.'

Well, no pressure, Humpybong 3D: we had to pray to save the world from destruction – as if we didn't have enough to contend with in Hanrahan and his Daleks. But somehow, we managed to get through both little and big lunch and beyond without the world being 'rooooned', to quote Hanrahan.

My mother would also recite the poem on occasion, for she loved an excuse to bung on a funny voice and 'Said Hanrahan' is a cracker for a bit of hammy noise. One such occasion was Boxing Day at my aunt's, who had a collection of what she referred to as 'Talking Poetry Records'. 'Said Hanrahan' appeared on a few.

The version she played the most was by an Australian actor called Leonard Teale, who we knew was famous because he was on *Homicide* on the telly and had bushy *Thunderbirds* eyebrows and a fruity adenoidal baritone voice. When he got to the part where Hanrahan would start with the bush Dalek bit, both my mum and aunty would boom, 'We'll all be rooooned!'

The poem is about a group of farmers who gather every Sunday after Mass to sit and chew a bit of bark and cast out their words of wisdom in regard to drought and rain and life in general.

One, a crusty old coot called Hanrahan, only sees ruination and never strays from his observation that disaster is imminent.

If there is drought, we'll all be 'rooned' before the year is out. When drought breaks and rains come, he moans about floods wiping all before them and how indeed we'll all be 'rooned'.

When lush green life-giving grass covers the district, it means there'll be bushfires for sure and more roon-nation.

So, a Hanrahan was a moaner, a doomsayer, a pessimist who looked at any situation and saw only disaster and gloom. 'No Hanrahans in our mob,' said my mother. Life in our family of five children would have been unruly enough, but having a Milly Moaner would have been too much to bear for all concerned.

And it was too easy, according to my parents, to see the sour side of things. Hanrahan no doubt would look at a glass of something nice – say, 'cornwater' – and see it being half empty when the reality for my parents was that there was more to enjoy in that glass, more to live for. The best 'cornwater' was to come.

For some unknown reason, whenever a tin of Golden Circle Sweet Corn was opened, the five of us McInnes offspring would go feral for a chance to drink the strained water from the tin. 'Cornwater' sounds like something hillbillies from the Ozarks would distil with their other moonshine, but that sweet yellow translucent broth from the bottom of the tin was like gold to us.

'Go easy with that,' said my mother as she shared the glass of cornwater around her brood as if she was a first mate doling out diminishing water rations to a lifeboat of shipwreck survivors.

Someone would invariably say, 'It's nearly gone,' and my mother would hold the glass out in front of the protester's face and boom, 'Look, see? It's really THERE!'

A glass half full. It made sense to us.

A friend of mine had an Uncle Barry, an old Brisbane boy, who used to say that when he felt in a bit of a grump, he'd jump on a City Cat and enjoy the bridges. There are sixteen bridges crossing the Brisbane River and they're more than just pieces of city infrastructure. My friend's uncle loved the bridges of Brisbane, loved how all the structures had their own personalities and were stories in themselves.

Uncle Barry had a kindred spirit in my mother, for she would see the graceful art-deco arches of the William Jolly

Bridge and turn that river crossing into a magical pathway to a happy place.

Remember, no Hanrahans in this mob. We're a glass half full mob, so get yourself on the William Jolly Bridge.

•

Just before the thing that we came to know as the Covid pandemic descended fully upon us all, I sat in an airport lounge, after missing yet another flight, and thought to myself, I'd best get to the William Jolly Bridge. Sometimes it's easy to be grumpy about things because there are so many reasons to be driven around the bend by what goes on in the world, it's seriously tempting not to get out of bed.

Ironically, at the time, I was looking down at a glass of beer I was halfway through drinking. Was it half full or half empty?

Sometimes you have to rely on hope. No Hanrahans in this mob.

I then made the mistake of paying attention to the television on the wall for a few moments. The stories were of unrelenting awfulness. A mother and her children fatally assaulted on the streets of Brisbane. A shot of floral tributes marking the site of the attack. And then a parade of doom-laden predictions about the Coronavirus that was just emerging.

Sitting nor far from me was a mother with three children. Young children. They were looking up at the television screen.

A shot of a plush toy amid the floral tributes.

'Mummy, a teddy,' said the little girl, pointing to the screen.

'Yes, a teddy,' the mother said softly, and then she reached out to her daughter and softly stroked her head.

They watched the screen while the mother gently stroked her daughter's hair. It was a warm and tender gesture. Almost protective.

'Why are they wearing masks?' the smaller of the boys asked the mother.

He was talking about the scenes of people from around the world with face masks, others in hazmat suits spraying disinfectants to try to contain the coronavirus.

'To try to keep themselves safe, to keep from getting sick,' said the mother. 'And to try to help other people from getting sick.'

'Will we get sick?' asked her daughter.

'I hope not, but we all get sick sometimes. Remember when you had a funny tummy?'

Her daughter grimaced and nodded. 'I couldn't have any hot chocolate,' she said.

'Well, you got better, didn't you? There are all types of getting sick, so we must be careful and hope for the best.'

'Will we have to wear masks?' asked her older son.

'We might,' said the mother. 'Sometimes we must wear things for a reason. We wear hats when we go outside so we don't get sunburnt; we might have to wear masks so we don't get sick.'

The kids thought and then the elder son asked if he could wear a Spiderman mask and the daughter said she would wear an Anna mask from *Frozen*.

The mother asked her youngest what mask he would wear. He thought for a moment and said he would wear a Jaffa mask.

The mother laughed and I did too. The little boy smiled.

The daughter said, 'Nothing is better than Jaffas.'

'Free Jaffas!' said the eldest boy.

'In big jars!' said the youngest. There were Jaffas by the tea station.

'I've loved Jaffas all my life and I'm six,' said the daughter.

'I love Jaffas more than you, and I'm seven,' said the eldest boy.

The youngest asked his mother if she would help him put on a mask if he had to wear one.

The mother said of course she would. Then she asked if they would like to go and get a Jaffa each.

The children ran off and the mother smiled. 'Jaffas will fix almost anything,' she said.

I wanted to say thank you to her.

Hope isn't just blind optimism – it's trusting, comforting and believing each other. It's protection and love.

I looked at my glass. And decided it was half full. I'd gotten across the William Jolly Bridge.

I often wondered how that mum and three kids navigated the Covid pandemic, with its lockdowns, isolation and home schooling. They seemed to be a glass half full mob and they had their own version of getting across the William Jolly Bridge – Jaffas can fix almost anything – so I assume they did okay.

But what to call the global pandemic that grew from those early scenes on the news broadcast?

The first time I became aware that the sterile and slightly terrifying term 'Coronavirus' was being given the Australian vernacular treatment was in, of all things, a bottle shop. I was there for some Irish gargle water and I dutifully stepped on my taped cross, adhering to the social distancing conditions, while a young fellow in his early twenties ahead of me ordered a 'carton of virus'.

Without a blink the bloke behind the counter went and fetched a carton of Corona beer, the Mexican extra pale lager that is popular with folk the customer's age.

I asked the bottle shop attendant if he'd heard Corona be called the 'virus' before. He nodded and said, 'Yep, virus is catching on.' And then he laughed a little.

The odd thing about the pandemic was that we had experts on it before we even understood what it actually was, before we could even put it into everyday terms.

And what experts they were, all gathered around, down on their heels, chewing the bark and Hanrahan-ing for all they were worth. The pandemic was made for Hanrahans, with doom-laden forecasts being uttered almost around the clock.

It struck me that the self-proclaimed pandemic expert Donald Trump would be an Olympic gold medallist at Hanrahan-ing. His pronunciation of 'rooned' would have squeezed more syllables out of that word than water from a squeezed sponge.

'Rooooned, very, very, very, very, very rooooooooooonnnned. It's a terrible, terrible thing. It really is.'

The pandemic was full of Hanrahans. Most were like the farmers in Pat Hartigan's poem, passing on thoughts that were a little bit obvious. Or, as my mother would have put it, stating the bleeding obvious.

And Hanrahan's pessimism, while comical in the poem, was displayed all too readily by the talking heads and experts trundled out throughout the pandemic. Their only satisfaction seemed to be that sooner or later their dire predictions would be proved right. At the very least, they made the William Jolly Bridge more difficult to cross.

Personally, I'd be very happy if I never heard from or saw an epidemiologist for a very long time, or a chief health officer.

Our language of this time seemed to be filled with acronyms – PCR, RAT, PPE, ICU. It's a sure sign of a crisis when capital letters are used on a daily basis. Forget about trying to understand what a polymerase chain reaction is, just call it a PCR. And a PCR is a sort of rapid antigen test, which became a RAT, but when you had one, people would say they had taken a RAT test. Repeating the word 'test' made it sound like baby talk, a rapid antigen test test.

The same for PPE, which sounded like someone being coy about urinating on the sly instead of being Personal Protective

Equipment. That sounds like a secreted gun or baseball bat under a counter.

ICU sounds like a segment from *Play School*, the pre-school educational show on the ABC. 'ICU!' says Big Ted to Jemima as he jumps out to give her a friendly fright, but Jemima doesn't want to see you, Big Ted, so that is why she grabs her baseball bat and belts you around your furry melon. And so Big Ted ends up in the Intensive Care Unit.

Best stick to the acronyms, that made for more efficient communication, even though nobody completely knew what it was that was being communicated.

•

People you knew only by sight and had never chatted to at length suddenly became people you would pass some of your Covid time with while doing the most mundane activities.

Outside the post office around the corner from my place, a gaggle of masked post office box owners would wait in dutiful social distancing mode to access their mail. A very nice woman who was the owner of two pleasantly behaved Afghan hounds called the daily news from Covid experts 'the revenge of the smart people'.

'The Covidians, I call them,' she said. 'Those people who were smart at uni, probably never did anything other than study and do well. People who we never heard from and never would have heard from until this bloody pandemic came along.'

They weren't Covidiots, she assured the masked gaggle. Covidiots were people who thought lockdowns and vaccinations and doing the right thing didn't apply to them.

The Lover of Afghan Hounds (LAH) seemed to sweep the masked gaggle with a look, just making sure we were in fact Covidiot-free. After she had satisfied herself that this was the case, she drew our attention to a perfect Covidiot case.

People like the owners of a large battleship of a car, an electric blue Range Rover that had been pulled over in front of the post office by a rather sly-looking police car lurking around the corner.

'Ahh,' said the LAH, and the dogs looked up at her and then back towards the blue battleship and then back to their owner. 'Covidiots! From Camberwell. Sneaking through the ring of steel, trying to pretend their weekender is their main residence. Caught out by the old rego check!'

For a pleasant person, she said this with a rather large slice of relish, as if she had just unmasked somebody practising witchcraft in Salem.

'Their weekender is three doors down from mine.' This, I think, was her way of explaining how she knew the Covidiots were from Camberwell. She added another clarification. 'I know Camberwell, taught there for years, and while there may have been some below average, Camberwellians certainly don't corner the Covidiot market. They're everywhere.'

Another in our group smiled through their mask and said, 'The old ring of steel.' It was a phrase used to describe a police presence marking the outer limits of Covid isolation zones and was supposed to be intimidating, but my masked colleague had a different view.

'Whenever I hear "ring of steel" it always sounds like it's some sort of incontinence product. Absorbent underwear.'

I laughed. There was a pause, and then the ring of steel (ROS) man said conspiratorially, 'You remember that astronaut?'

I was a little perplexed for a moment, and then laughed again.

ROS laughed too. 'You reckon she wore a ring of steel?'

'Quite possibly.'

How long, I wondered, had ROS waited to air his absorbent underwear claims? To find a fellow traveller along the channel of ephemeral popular culture and tacky titbits?

Well, I was in.

All he needed was to set the spark with the words, 'Remember *that* astronaut?' Not the first man on the moon, or the first human in space or all the other brave people who had travelled beyond earth's boundaries, but *that* astronaut. It was one of those stories you never forgot, emblazoned in magazines and on news sites, and the butt of a thousand jokes.

Lisa Nowak, a NASA astronaut, reportedly made use of a MAG (a maximum absorbency garment) when, along with wearing a bad wig, black coat and fake glasses, she drove over 1500 kilometres across the United States to an airport carpark in order to pepper-spray and scare the living daylights out of another woman. The woman Nowak confronted had just begun dating another astronaut whom Nowak had dated in the past.

Apparently, when she approached the woman, the intended victim said, 'Lisa Nowak? Hello! What are you doing here?'

What a thing to be known for: the astronaut who crewed a space shuttle then wore a bad disguise and a nappy in a lovelorn fit of violent passion.

'The ring of steel will protect and give confidence! Go about your life activities secure in the knowledge you have no leakage,' said ROS. 'Just don't get caught by the Wallopers!'

We both laughed.

'Yes,' said the LAH, 'Covidians are the clever people we have to listen to.' We all watched as the police took notes on an iPad and wrote out a form for the owners of the blue battleship.

All this had made some sort of sense to me, for all the chief health officers, CHOs, certainly looked like they had studied very diligently at uni and were the sort of people I might have tried to cadge study notes off back in the day.

Now each day they appeared before the press to give numbers and facts. Talking patiently and endlessly, sometimes awkwardly and uncomfortably in the limelight they never sought.

ROS asked me, 'Who do you think would be smarter? An astronaut, a Covidian or a former high school principal?'

He nodded towards the LAH.

I said I supposed they were all pretty smart.

ROS nodded. 'Yes, I suppose they all are.' And then he laughed a little. 'And any one of us could end up wearing a ring of steel.'

All of us, despite how smart we might be, could be terribly silly at times.

As the LAH moved off towards her turn at the post boxes she said resignedly, 'Covidians may have an air of smugness about them but I suppose we just have to listen and do as we're told.'

A self-described 'grumpy old coot' (GOC) from down the road muttered that that sort of talk was 'rich, coming from someone who walks with a couple of camel trader's mutts'.

I assumed he was referring to the pleasant dogs and Afghan camel traders from Australia's colonial past.

Somebody else in the masked gaggle had heard our exchange.

'They are odd dogs, aren't they? Lovely but odd. So hairy.'

I heard myself say, 'They were always in fashion back in the day. In flashy magazines.'

The GOC chimed in again. 'In *Cosmopolitan*. Shampoo ads.'

My sisters all read *Vogue*, *Cleo* and *Cosmopolitan* so there were a fair few copies to sift through in the home I grew up in.

My mother was slightly suspicious of some of the 'young woman's content', quite unlike the *Australian Women's Weekly* or the disturbingly austere English *Woman's Weekly*, which seemed as if it was printed in the days of wartime rationing. My father had no truck with my sisters' magazines and thought they were the 'rags with the nude coots in them'. Centrefolds of semi-naked men.

He came across me whipping though a *Cosmopolitan* on the back verandah one afternoon and hurried off to confront my mother in the kitchen.

I followed not too far behind and did my best to keep out of sight.

'What does your bloody son want it for? What's he up to?' whispered my father.

'Oh wake up,' my mother whispered back. 'He's looking at the underwear advertisements.'

My father stared.

His mind worked. He did something with his eyebrows which meant that he needed more information.

'Women's underwear ads.' My mother's whisper could be heard in distant Sandgate it was so theatrical.

My father's eyebrows rose through the atmosphere and he tilted his head. This could be serious.

'Oh, you stupid man.' My mother was still whispering, but it was like something from a Victorian melodrama. 'He's looking at the women. In their smalls.'

'Ohhh,' my father said loudly in an elongated sigh of relief. 'He's just having a gawp. That's all right then.'

Well, it wasn't really, but the thought made me laugh as I stood in my mask outside the post office.

The GOC turned his mask towards me when he heard me laugh.

'I remember my girlfriend buying the shampoo because she liked those dogs.'

Again I heard my own masked tones. 'My dad called them hairdresser's hounds.'

Dad would call them hairdresser's hounds because, in his eyes, the dogs were ornate and not really that practical. It didn't mean they weren't nice dogs, just decorative and a little ephemeral – like hairdressers, as opposed to barbers, in his view. A good old kelpie cross was a barber's dog, a working practical animal, and Afghans were hairdresser's pets.

The GOC said almost wistfully to himself, 'Bobo Faulkner.'

Nobody said anything for a moment. Then I said, 'Sorry?'

'Bobo Faulkner,' said the GOC dreamily. 'She did Cool Charm ads in *Cosmopolitan*.'

'Her hair smelt lovely,' the GOC continued. 'My girlfriend's,' he added, 'not Bobo Faulkner's.'

•

It was only after I'd returned home and done a spot of googling that I worked out who or what Bobo Faulkner was. She had been a model, actress, television presenter and entrepreneur in the late 1960s and the 1970s, a time when the GOC would have been a young lad.

Whether Bobo Faulkner did shampoo ads with Afghans wasn't raised, but the way the GOC had intoned her name had a rather wistful hint to it.

It was very still that morning, although the breeze from the bay played through the big gum trees just enough to sigh gently, and the grumpy old coot hadn't seemed that grumpy as he'd softly recalled a moment from his life. Bobo Faulkner was more an emotional state than a person, some long-ago ephemeral touchstone to his life. A shared moment with somebody he had cared about, somebody he probably wasn't expecting to recall as he went to wait in line, at the appropriate social distance, to access his post office box.

It struck me as being quite lovely.

Maybe he'd told his girlfriend all those years ago how lovely her hair smelt, or maybe he just remembered it for himself.

It seemed to me that to 'Bobo Faulkner' was to rummage through your mind and memory, maybe muse a little and come up with some moment from your past. A pandemic can do that to you. We all Bobo Faulknered one way or the other.

The odd thing, I recall now, is that I had gone to collect mail from my post office box almost every day, and had seen most of the people who used to make up the MGG (Masked Gaggle Gang) each time, but I have never spoken to them since and they have never spoken to me. A case of a CPCE (Covid Pandemic Conversation Experience). Although I do get the occasional nod from the ROS and the GOC.

The thing I realised though is that if you begin a bit of Bobo Faulknering, it can quickly morph into a bout of COFAing.

(The propensity for all kinds of people to descend into the use of acronyms was another unanticipated pandemic gift.)

As a fully paid-up member of the COFA, Conservative Old Farts Association, I admit sometimes I may be capable of mumbling on in a grumpy manner. Or I can be, as I've been informed by those close to me, a calamitously annoying bore, as near enough to the *Looney Tunes* legend Foghorn Leghorn in human form as one might find. And I know what we all went through was wretched and we should all be as kind and as generous to each other as we possibly can be now.

Having laid all that out, though, the next time I hear a politician, radio host, qualified expert or faux expert declare that we are living through 'unprecedented times' I will pull what's left of my hair out.

I think it was an old British Imperialist politician called Joseph Chamberlain who came up with the saying 'May you live in interesting times'. It was supposed to be a half curse. Well, he should've tried living in 'unprecedented times'.

During the first Easter of Covid, for my sins, I was listening to the radio where that most dreaded of Hanrahan creatures, a UTE (unprecedented times expert) was giving views about how to get through the Easter break.

We had to be kind to ourselves, we were told, and recognise what might be impacting on us. And that was that. Ourselves. Just us. Just you. Just me. Think about yourself. Personal responsibility is one thing; selfishness is another.

It was Easter. A time of sacrifice, compassion and redemption. A time of thinking about other people. Of understanding none of us is perfect, that some of us may be in different circumstances and react differently, some of us may not always be at our best.

As my old man was fond of saying, if we keep an eye on each other, cut people a bit of slack, and make sure none are left behind, we'll be right. Or is that too Foghorn Leghorn?

Bobo Faulknering can lead you down all sorts of rabbit holes, and indeed one man's Bobo Faulknering was a case of 'jumping in the DeLorean' to another, and engaging in a bit of mental time travel a la *Back to the Future*.

My Doc Brown was my grand pal PB, who claimed creator's rights for 'jumping in the DeLorean'. He rang up once and wanted to know how iso was going. Meaning he wanted to know how I was going, which was a friend checking on another friend and using vernacular to let you know it was all okay.

I like the word 'iso' because it has an old Australian feel to it. It echoes back to the ice deliverymen of a previous Australia and their cry of 'Ice-oh!' – both a sign of their arrival with the blocks of ice they delivered and of relief that a vital service and necessity was at hand. Blocks were used to put in ice boxes, a precursor to refrigerators, so at least a minimum of food sanitation and comfort was provided. Or in other words, your chops could stay cold instead of going off.

It signalled a tougher time in Australia, perhaps, during the Great Depression – a time of less wealth, less privilege and less entitlement.

So 'social isolation' became 'iso'. No big deal, just something we had to get through. And with a little help along the way, iso was a cinch!

Well, that was the theory. Mostly we put up with it, but there was lots of whining and whingeing, which might have made our more stoic forebears wonder about us.

During that phone call with PB he very nearly ended a decades-long friendship with me because I innocently praised a ham, cheese and tomato toastie for making iso a little more palatable.

'Mate,' he said, 'in all the years I have known you, I have NEVER heard you refer to the inestimable toasted sanger as a "toastie"! What's going on, mate? You in trouble or something?

'It's a bloody toasted sanger, mate. EOS!' (End of story – another acronym, complete with an exclamation mark, apparently.)

'Don't you understand?' he continued. 'We DO NOT alter the slang terms of anything in Australia once they have been established. Sure, we put an "ie" on the end of some things –'

I interrupted. 'Like vernacular becoming vernac and then vernac-ie?'

'You nong, vernac-ie sounds like one of John Travolta's mates in *Grease*. Stop showboating. You can "ie" but not if they have a beaut name already. Are you with me? We can come up with new words, but you can't renovate a perfectly good word. With me?'

'Go on,' I replied.

'Look, you drongo, it's hardly a bloody insult if I call you a drongie, is it? Sounds bloody ridiculous. I dunno what game you're playin', son, but if you call it a toastie next time I see you, fair dinkum . . .'

I asked PB if he was deliberately talking like Chips Rafferty, the old Australian string-bean actor of the mid-twentieth century, or whether he'd been out in the sun too long.

'Adding a dash of colour to my conversation,' he replied.

I paused and then suggested drongie had a French ring to it and could pass for a fancy or foppish drongo.

'Ah, *chérie*, you should see how the drongie eats his toastie,' I said in a bad French accent, channelling my best inner Pepé Le Pew, the *Looney Tunes* romantic French skunk.

'Stick to Foghorn Leghorn, Big Fella, it comes more naturally.'

PB returned to his defence of Australian vernac.

'Drongie's not a word. Never was, never will be.'

I suggested that iso was going well for him.

'It has its moments,' was his reply. And that was true for all of us.

PB, however, had come up with the idea of concocting lists of things to pass the time. Covid listings, he called them. He would send around a subject and away we would all go.

The best ten Mental as Anything songs. The top ten K-tel products. The top ten places where movie stars would buy lunch on the Redcliffe Peninsula. Two James Bonds made the list. Roger Moore eating fish and chips at The Honey Pot Snack Bar tickled my fancy because Honey Pot sounds like a Bond girl from Roger's era. 'Go easy on the chicken salt, Honey Pot!' intones Roger as he reaches for a bit of sophisticated carbohydrate in the form of a chip. 'And remember, chicken salt is shaken, not stirred.'

Sean Connery apparently snacked at an infamous takeaway in Woody Point that insisted on placing a ring of pineapple on everything that was put between two bits of bread.

PB was adamant that he was present on a Saturday night when somebody complained they didn't want a ring of pineapple on their hamburger. The complainant brought the burger to the counter. The proprietor said fair enough, opened the burger, took careful aim and pierced the pineapple ring with his index finger then carried it to an open tin of Golden Circle Pineapple Rings and dropped it back in the tin. He then placed one half of the hamburger on top of the other and handed it back to the customer with a friendly, 'All done, there you go.'

Sean Connery must have thought the Goldfinger snack was more Gold-en-Circle-Finger.

And then there was Arnold Schwarzenegger ordering a sausage roll from the bakery from Midway shopping centre because, like Arnie's famous line from *Terminator*, 'I'll be back,' the snag roll had a miraculous ability to keep returning to the consumer in various belching forms while it was being digested.

PB asked if I had any list suggestions.

'Top ten toasties,' I said.

There was a pause and PB muttered. 'Come to think of it, you really are a bloody drongie. Stop fucking with the vernac–ie.'

•

The strange thing about a touch of the Bobo Faulkners, or jumping in the DeLorean or whatever you'd like to call it, was that having the time to have a bit of a think about moments from your life could be a surprising side benefit of the pandemic. Thinking about being wrong, for example.

Most of us are wrong occasionally – perhaps even a little more than occasionally, but who's counting? I never realised how much admitting you are wrong might mean until the other week.

I've been wrong about so many things, it doesn't bear thinking about. Politicians, cricketers, rugby players, having a flutter on a sure-fire bet, thinking a sky-blue skivvy and a pair of Stubbies shorts would be just the thing to impress a potential date at a party back in the 1980s at a Sydney harbourside mansion.

Wrong about a lot of things.

I was having a lovely time fishing recently, waiting for a nibble, listening to the gentle lap of waves, when I remembered an argument I'd had with a woman years ago. She'd said one of her favourite sounds was of waves, because to her it nearly always meant happiness.

Years ago we had argued over some decision in a play we were both in, and because I had the loudest voice, I won.

Even when it was done my way, I thought she had probably been right. Well, she was. I was wrong.

I had an acute case of the 'feels', being slightly moved emotionally by the heedless wrong I might have caused. Another time I might have felt a bit guilty, sworn at myself, and got on with what I was doing. But a case of the 'feels' brought on by a Bobo Faulkner caused me to reach for my phone.

I texted. 'Listening to waves. Thought of you and that argument we had. Sorry. I was wrong. It should have been done your way.'

I didn't get a reply until later when I was cleaning my catch.

'Thank you. After the year I've had, someone saying they were wrong and apologising means a lot to me. Thanks, you big plonker.'

It struck me that the return text was full of surprise, humour, generosity and grace.

Apologising for an old wrong can mean a lot.

The things a bit of Bobo Faulknering can teach you.

I went back to cleaning my catch.

CHAPTER 3
TESTING TIMES

One day during the pandemic, I headed off to get a couple of coffees from a place around the corner that made lovely brews. It was drizzling slightly and, even though I like rain, being caught in it can be a hassle.

Never mind, I thought, I could wait in the café.

Not on this day. It was only doing takeaways because new concrete was being laid on the footpath outside. There was a sodden little group waiting in the drizzle like shags on rocks, hunched a little and just chinning the wet.

I nodded to a few fellow shags, made sure I wasn't pushing in and was told by another shag to take his place at the little window with a good-natured old Australian phrase indicating that no offence had been given and none had been taken, 'No, you're right.'

A cement truck was emptying its contents into the formwork of the footpath and three workers were distributing the concrete and then smoothing it evenly, one barking out directions to the fellow in the truck. Shouts of 'Forward!' echoed around the front of the café. The man who was shouting had a loud and sure voice even though he was wearing a face mask.

I listened to the command and laughed a little and said to nobody in particular that it reminded me of being in the army cadets at school, with teachers playing dress-ups in military outfits and roaring at a motley mob of us early teenage droobs.

I gave my order to a barista who looked like he'd stepped out of a hipster catalogue and, as he added the coffees to his list, he laughed. 'Cadets? Old-school, my friend.'

A woman who was dressed head to foot in activewear asked me, 'Did you see much action?'

Some other shags chuckled.

I admitted that we weren't much chop. 'We were so hopeless that we weren't allowed to march in the Anzac Day Parade because it looked like we were trying to take the mickey.'

'Take the mickey?' asked the catalogue hipster barista.

'Make fun of,' said another shag.

'More old-school,' said the catalogue hipster barista.

The woman in activewear laughed and said that her brother had been in the cadets at his school and that, 'The most dangerous thing about them was their acne.'

This made the rest of us shags laugh. Along with the catalogue hipster barista. He tugged at his face mask. 'These things,' he said to himself, but everybody else hummed in agreement.

The man with the loud and sure voice yelled again. 'FORWARD!'

Again, the cement truck rolled slowly and surely.

'You know,' the catalogue hipster barista said all of a sudden, 'I always wondered what it would be like to live through an "age". You know?'

'How do you mean?' I said.

'An age, a thing, a time. Like maybe, you guys –' he pointed to us masked shags, '– lived through the Cold War?'

'The Cold War?' a shag said slightly indignantly.

Nobody said anything. The Cold War seemed to belong to History with a capital H, and that meant long, long ago. Stalin. The Korean War. Mao. JFK.

Well, I was born after big Jack died. And then ... the Vietnam War, Nixon, detente, the Trip to China, Class 3D praying for peace (what did happen to Miss Law?), I could have gone on. But no, we had all lived through the Cold War. How hadn't we noticed that? The catalogue hipster barista was right.

'Yeah,' said the catalogue hipster barista, 'learnt about that in history at school.'

A woman in a neatly homemade mask made a little self-deprecating scoffing sound.

I did a quick bit of mental arithmetic. When did the Cold War start? Just after World War II, and it ended – when? When the Soviet Union collapsed. Early '90s; 1991.

I looked up and noticed all we shags had the same slightly furrowed brow, thinking. And working out that we had in fact all lived through a part of the Cold War. The arse end.

Nobody said anything until I said, 'Well, I know I lived through the age of disco.'

'Yeah, right, the Cold War,' the catalogue hipster barista said. 'That was disco. We saw it all on that song.'

Some shags groaned. Billy Joel. 'We Didn't Start the Fire'.

'Yeah,' said the catalogue hipster barista, and then he added, 'Age of disco? You still got the moves?'

'On the right night,' I said.

'Or when you get enough coffee.' The catalogue hipster barista was enjoying himself.

'My uncle was talking of living through AIDS – even though AIDS is something people still get, but he lived through AIDS when it was everywhere. You know the thing.'

Yes, I thought, it was the thing. I wouldn't have been much older than the catalogue hipster barista's uncle then. Probably younger, in fact.

'Must have been so scary.'

I remember being at footy training once when I was younger than the catalogue hipster barista, having beers in the change room and someone asking where 'Nunny' was. Nunny had the flu, was feeling off.

'Weak as,' said a prop.

'He is a winger so I hope it's not the arse flu,' said somebody else. And people laughed. Not all, but enough. It was when AIDS was a 'gay thing' or it happened to somebody else, before everybody knew it wasn't just a 'gay thing', before it became an epidemic. Yes, AIDS was certainly a thing.

And now we were all living through another thing. History, I thought, is the distilled version of all the messy shit you live through, and then one day when you are trying to get a coffee that distillation is presented to you. And at first you don't remember it. Strange. But it does give you perspective.

The catalogue hipster barista was finishing up a macchiato. 'So now we're all here,' he said, 'living in the age of . . .' He paused and we all waited.

'The age of . . . face jocks!' And he pointed to the mask on his face.

Nobody said anything and then we all laughed.

I had read online that you could make an effective face mask out of two pairs of a particular brand of undies that were cut up with the two crotches sewn together to provide a high level of protection. The creation was called a 'jock mask' and I supposed it was a distant cousin of the face jocks.

I had a crack at making the jock mask but decided to forgo the brand undies in favour of a pair from Kmart. Perhaps because I went for the cheaper option, or perhaps because my sewing skills were lacking, what I ended up with wasn't so much a jock mask as a cross between a frontier bandit and Claude Rains in *The Invisible Man*.

Once when I walked in to pay for a tank of petrol at a 7-Eleven servo the bloke behind the counter said it was taking a while for him to get used to people wearing 'heart-starters'.

I asked what he meant, and he explained a 'heart-starter' was a customer's face mask.

'First couple of times they gave me a fright. I didn't know whether I was going to be robbed. It was like, do I reach for the baseball bat or press the panic button or call the police or just ask which pump?'

And then there was the time I headed into the local supermarket behind a tradie. Just as he was about to step into the shop he looked up and saw his reflection: he was maskless. He uttered an oath, felt in his pockets, groaned again, turned and headed for his ute.

The next time I saw him was in the spice aisle wearing a welding helmet. I laughed and said, 'Good effort.'

He replied with a muffled, 'You got to be able to improvise with this bloody thing!'

A kid packing shelves nearby was laughing. He looked up and said it was like having the Mandalorian shopping in the store. The tradie was obviously a fan of the *Star Wars* universe because he looked at the kid and said, 'Boba Fett please, young fella – original trilogy.'

The kid laughed.

A week later I walked through the aisles again and the same kid was telling another shelf packer, 'You've got to wear your Boba Fett properly or you'll get toasted by the floor manager.'

Somehow a face mask had become a Boba Fett, thanks to a lateral-thinking tradie. Priceless.

Back to face jocks. The woman with the homemade face mask – not a face jock, I might add – laughed and said, 'Haven't heard that before.'

'Yeah,' said the catalogue hipster barista. 'Looks like a little man-package there.' He made a circling gesture with his index and middle fingers over his mask. 'It's a little gender-specific,' he added, 'but yeah, fun name.'

'Not to be confused with dick nose,' said the woman with the homemade face mask.

This was a derogatory term for a person who wore a mask over their mouth but pulled down the mask so their nose hung out over the top. 'Just defeats the purpose of wearing the mask.'

Those would be part of the Covidiot family, I supposed.

The catalogue hipster barista nodded. 'One of the Aunties,' he said.

'Forward!' yelled the workman. The truck rolled forward again.

'Aunty Maskers, Aunty Vaxxers, Aunty Lockdowns.'

I laughed. 'The mad aunts!'

'Yeah,' said the catalogue hipster barista, 'but you've got to remember they're still family!'

Where would you start?

Courtesy of the pandemic we now have the word 'jab' as an all-purpose term for the application of a vaccine for Covid.

The jab meant we witnessed a flurry of our political leaders with arms bared smiling happily, making a 'V' for vaccination/victory, all to reassure us there was nothing to worry about, no pain, much gain, and by getting the jab we were doing our civic duty.

Thankfully, our pollies were modest, unlike some of their European counterparts who flashed the rig while getting the jab.

Some rigs were serviceable but, say what you want about Scomo, Albo and co, they saved us from their middle-aged paddocks by wearing t-shirts.

Flash your V-signs, smile, call it whatever you want, but needles are never fun.

I hate them. Always have, from school inoculations, vaccines for overseas, dental anaesthetic and the odd sporting painkiller, I've never warmed to the needle.

People smiling makes it worse. I remember my son, now a fully grown Clydesdale, going off as an unbearably cute baby for a shot. Me, the nurse, the doctor were all smiling, full of good humour; him the centre of attention.

His baby face broke into a beautiful smile the size of a Cavendish banana and then the needle struck and he looked at me with such anguished betrayal I felt rather guilty.

Anyway, he got a treat, I'm sure. Along with protection and good health.

Calling the needle 'the jab' won't convince anti-vaxxers to trust the science or soften the needle's point, but hats off for trying. The jab has an old-world quality, and I can imagine

Ray Warren using his most baroque tones to pronounce it across the ages.

I like to think of Ray warbling away, repeating the words a teacher said to us in my early years of high school before an inoculation.

'This isn't just for you, you know. It's for all of us. You're keeping safe and growing, that's what life is all about.'

And then there was the girl who told me how her mum had told her not to worry about the odd little round scar on her arm, courtesy of a jab, because it wasn't a scar but a 'Good Health Medal'.

My old man would have called the jab a personal Everest. I thought about him and Aunty Vaxxers on hearing about the recent anniversary of some Kiwi bloke called Ed reaching the top of the world's highest mountain. Sir Edmund Hillary, of course, a wonderful human being. Many had tried before and come up short. It was heralded as an example of the triumph of the human spirit. Almost unimaginable. Since that day Kiwi Ed's been joined by 5788 other examples of the triumph of the human spirit.

A woman at a work do told me that she had a relative who'd climbed Everest. An American dentist. 'He's some sort of uncle or something.'

'Oh,' I said. 'Do you like mountaineering?'

'No, I get a nosebleed going up an escalator, but he's a useful conversation starter.'

The triumph of the human spirit as a conversation starter. Not bad.

There's been other dentists, as well as doctors, engineers, tradies, a car salesperson, gardeners, a yak herder and even a barman who've climbed the tallest mountain in the world.

Once unimaginable, but nowadays the mountain has become a bit of a highway and is strewn with the rubbish and detritus of those who've attempted the climb. But why? Why do people want to climb Everest?

'Because it's there.' That's the quote on those wretched inspirational posters you see, usually in accountants' offices. And yes, accountants have climbed Mount Everest.

As a kid, I remember people running ridiculous distances, like shuffling Cliff Young, or swimming ridiculous distances, like a fellow called Des Renford from Sydney who was always swimming the English Channel, nineteen times in all.

'He wants to get another bloody hobby, old Des,' my mum used to say. 'He should try canasta.'

There was a young student from Redcliffe High called Jenny Anderson who swam from Tangalooma to the mainland. She became a distance swimmer of great note who swam the English Channel as well.

I remember coming downstairs in my PJs on the morning her feat was splashed across the paper.

'Why would she do that?' I whined.

My old man looked at me. 'Good question, coming from a droob who's got his PJs on inside out. Why?'

I stared.

'Because she's a human being. That's what we do. Have a crack. Climb a mountain or swim a bay, split the atom or be a good citizen. We've all got our Mount Everests, that's why we have a crack. It's a good thing to give yourself an Everest, big or small.'

I always wince and carry on when I get needles and will do almost anything not to come into contact with the bloody things. Yet I remembered my old man's words about good citizenship and having a crack when I went and got my Covid jab.

Maybe to some a needle's not much of a personal Everest, but I felt as if Kiwi Ed and my old man would approve.

The catalogue hipster barista was right about the Aunties, though. We were all the same family and I suppose everyone had a right to their views.

Although the Auntys gave a bad name to the 'Cookers', those who dive into the world of cooking up conspiracies and alternative facts.

These days, conspiracy theories have been ruined by becoming too serious – the stakes are too high. Thankfully, there's always that great leveller: the Australian sense of humour. That's where the Cookers live and thrive.

I miss old, nonsensical Cooker conspiracy theories: Elvis sightings, British Royals being reptilian aliens, UFOs landing in Kippa-Ring, and that old favourite – mind control.

An old housemate during my uni days 'knew' why dropped buttered toast always landed on the buttered side. Physics provides explanations – the effects of gravity, angles at which the toast is dropped, and so on – but my housemate knew the truth.

'Mind control!'

Who was behind it?

'The Queensland Butter Board!' was the answer. 'They don't want to lose out to margarine.'

His source? 'Some bloke at the rugby club, he's a farmer, or related to one, or something.'

Some bloke. An irrefutable source.

According to this flatmate, Wrigley's sticks of chewing gum with lists of letters on the inside packaging weren't part of a competition where a full alphabet wins a prize, but mind control carried out by the Masons, the Vatican and ASIO. Maybe they each had dibs on different flavours.

The best mind control theory was proffered by an uncle of a friend. She said he blamed the old Expo Sky Needle laser show for affecting the egg-laying patterns of his chooks.

'It meddles with their minds, so who knows what it does to us?' she told me.

'Excuse me while I lay an egg,' I said to my mate, and she replied, 'There's nothing like having an uncle as a chook cooker!'

Now we were all living through an 'age' as the catalogue hipster barista had said, and people from the prime minister down were trying to call upon the spirit of older generations to give us all a bit of a gee-up. The Anzacs, those who won the peace after World War II – all who'd gone before and who'd given us a template for how to behave.

So it was a bit confounding when you looked at the panic-buying stripping shelves, the hoarding of toilet paper, the self-obsessed fury directed to staff of supermarkets and other shoppers.

I never thought I'd see signs on empty shelves in markets saying 'Aggressive and abusive behaviour will not be tolerated. Our team is here to help, not to be hurt.'

So much for the Anzac spirit.

I know a carer who helps some of the more disadvantaged members of our society who are inflicted with disability and chronic health issues. One morning, she took a client for the early-morning shopping hour created to serve the needs of the most vulnerable shoppers. Unsurprisingly, there was a crush and her client couldn't understand the push and shove.

He became agitated, so his carer took the long way round to the toilet paper. Plodding down the long aisles, it took an age to get to the section where so many had headed before them. When they finally made it, the shelves were empty. No toilet paper.

The carer and her client stood there. 'Oh no, all gone,' said the client in a wavering voice. He found it hard not to have certainty. Empty shelves worried him. His carer reached to comfort him, but she turned when she heard a voice. A tiny old woman walking with the aid of a cane.

The old woman came up to them slowly, saying, 'Now, that's no good. Is he upset?'

The carer said her client was.

'Now, that's no good. Don't be upset, love.' And the old woman proffered her basket. 'I've some rolls here, see?'

The carer wasn't sure what that meant, until it dawned upon her that the old woman was offering the toilet rolls to her client. The carer began to protest but the woman said, 'I'll only need a roll or two and he can have the rest. You can have some, son, don't be upset.'

The client was silent. And then he smiled and said thank you as well as he could.

The carer thought she might cry but as the old woman walked with them towards the checkouts she said, 'We're in it together, love, don't be upset. We'll go old-school and share.'

Sometimes we're small and petty. And sometimes we can be mighty. Good to remember.

•

Back at the café, we shags stood and waited while another command of 'Forward!' boomed out. I watched as the surface was smoothed over with sure and even graceful strokes of trowels and floats.

As a kid, I loved watching things being done. Maybe roadworks on the way home from school, builders on a site, people in a bakery, my mum making something in the kitchen.

I looked up and snuck a peek at the other shags. All were looking at the workers.

One shag said, 'It's sort of mesmerising, isn't it?'

A few nodded.

It was reassuring to see people being so competent, I thought. Those workers on the footpath creating order, getting things done. I liked it. And I looked again at the other shags, waiting in a good-natured orderly manner even though we all had places to be and things to get on with. I liked that too.

Competency, order and good cheer. Who wouldn't be buoyed by those things?

Australia, by and large, is a pretty bloody good place to be, where there's generally a competent way we go about things.

It's important to be reminded of that and perhaps I wasn't alone in my thinking. The catalogue hipster barista nodded at the workers as he gave me my coffees. He must have seen me looking at the jar on the counter, for he opened it and put a Jaffa on top of the coffees. 'Those guys make me feel good. Artists. And I like that things are getting done.'

'That's a bit old-school,' said another shag.

'Maybe, maybe not,' said the smiling catalogue hipster barista. 'But sometimes old-school is just what we need.'

Well, there you go.

●

After the last of the lockdowns, I was in a play that was one of the first productions to go into full rehearsal. An attempt to get back to a new normal. The play was good. It was a bit rough because the author had died before he could really finish it off, but it was a heartfelt celebration of what he loved doing when he wasn't writing plays: singing in community choirs. The director was a lovely bloke who was a great friend of the author and wanted to do justice to his pal's last work. The cast were all nice people who were enjoying the rehearsal. And then there was me. A fully paid-up member of COFA, remember. Face jocks were optional, but we had to keep a safe distance in rehearsals, so it was a little like a school play where everybody in the class was shy and awkward and didn't want to stand too close to somebody else. We did a lot of sitting at the rehearsal table.

People did a lot of talking. And some more talking. At times the rehearsals seemed like a bad episode of *Q&A*. Lots of opinions and monologues and not much listening.

It was just one of those things, I suppose, everyone getting used to being back working with other people. Or perhaps I was in a grump. I wasn't feeling that great, not since the second week of rehearsals. Or maybe it was the weekend. Or it was the party.

It was the party. A belated sixtieth. Even more ominously, it was an industry party, which meant a lot of people had just come back from somewhere else. A festival in Berlin and a conference on the Gold Coast. It was, in the words of the Man Who Should Be Famous – an eminent legal figure who is always being mistaken for famous actors like Bryan Cranston, Guy Pearce and even Brad Pitt – the perfect place to get the 'Spicy Cough'. In other words, Covid.

The Man Who Should Be Famous is fun because even though he has a serious job, the fact that people mistake him so often for a number of celebrities is almost unbelievable. True to form, just before I saw him at the do, a well-known director cried out with familiarity, 'Oh here's Guy!' And this director had worked with the real Guy Pearce.

The Man Who Should Be Famous's wife laughed with me when I told her and she said, 'This is new! People usually only think he's somebody else when we're on holiday. But I suppose it's a social occasion, so that counts.'

I asked the Man Who Should Be Famous why he thought our chances of getting the Spicy Cough were high. Just a feeling, he said. I admitted that I had a feeling as well.

'Somebody at work told me the other day that the best way not to get Covid is to believe you aren't going to get it. To be a NO-vid. A person who just wills it won't happen.'

The Man Who Should Be Famous looked at me in a very judicial way.

'It was an actor that said it,' I said, as if I was giving evidence against one of my own. Which was exactly what I was doing.

'I thought it was ridiculous,' I added.

Another look from Brad Pitt.

'I thought that as soon as I thought that I was trashing some poor sod's nonsense, I was bound to get it.' I shrugged my shoulders. Was I a sub-branch member of the Covidiot Association for sprouting such nonsense?

Bryan Cranston looked at me and said, 'That doesn't sound like a rational or a logical thought process.'

I admitted he was right, and asked him why he had a feeling.

Guy Pearce took a deep breath and looked at me keenly. 'I just thought, we are bound to catch something with so many unwashed and suspicious arty-farty creative types in one airless room.'

There was a pause and we both laughed.

We both caught Covid that night.

I had my suspicions because I began to feel even more grumpier in the rehearsals and going into work one morning on a train, I decided to do another test.

On a train? Things had changed quite a bit during this pandemic, so much so that another actor working on another play at the theatre company told me over coffee one morning that we had nothing more to worry about because Covid couldn't give us any more surprises and was now something we could understand.

I did manage to ask where the actor had heard this theory.

'Oh,' she waved airily, 'I can't remember, on some podcast I think, or someone told me who'd listened to a podcast. Or something.'

Christ, I thought as I headed into work on a sparsely populated train. I sat and thought to myself, I have one of those tests in my bag. A RAT test: a Rapid Antigen Test test.

We had all been given boxes of tests to do each week and I decided to do one right then on the train. Why not? People did all manner of things on trains — read, scroll through their phones, daydream, listen to music. I saw someone doing their nails once.

I managed to apply the test without removing my face jocks.

I watched and saw the two little red lines appear. Positive.

I rang the company and was sent for another test at a hospital, a PCR test.

There used to be a news conference announcing the number of Covid cases each day, which prompted two sisters I knew to indulge in games of Corona Lotto. The two would wager packets of their favourite lollies on what the figures might amount to and would tabulate the results over a 'vino quarantino': a glass of wine or two imbibed during lockdown.

We were a long way down the track now. I was told to go to the testing area of a major hospital where I met a woman from pathology with a N95 face mask. She was friendly and up for a chat as she showed me the way.

'These bloody things . . .' She tugged at her heavy-duty mask. 'They are bloody awful, aren't they? Still, won't need them soon, hopefully.'

I asked why.

'Oh, just things running their course.' She tugged again and said, 'We can get back to a face mask being some goo from Priceline that you're given on Mother's Day as a present to smear and let coagulate on your face.'

She stopped and pointed to an upturned milk crate. It was yellow. I looked at it and then looked back to her. She seemed to be smiling behind the mask, if you looked at her eyes.

'This is where we test you,' she said.

'Here?' My voice must have had a certain tone because she added, 'Yes, it's a bit cramped for space inside.'

An ambulance drove slowly past and parked. Beside it was a white prison van from the remand centre. A prisoner was being led into the hospital.

I supposed I should sit down.

Not far away, people stood in little clumps. This was the smoking area. A man with speed dealers' sunglasses and a black cap and AC/DC t-shirt was taking in the sight of me and the departing prisoner.

A nurse in full protective clothing came out of the glass doors and headed towards me. I presumed he had passed the prisoner.

The smoking AC/DC man said casually, 'Good day for it.'

I like that expression, a classic piece of time-filling banter. What 'it' was didn't matter, but it was a good day for whatever 'it' was — which, in my case, was getting a swab shoved up my nostrils and around the inside of my mouth.

'Yeah, not bad,' I replied to AC/DC man.

The nurse did what he had to do.

'Got the Rona, Big Fella?' said the smoking AC/DC man. The nurse was asking me who I was and going through checks.

'The Rona, yeah, the old lager lungs, beery breath. The Rona.' AC/DC man blew a few smoke rings.

He was quiet as the nurse swabbed me and then almost as a matter of course, as if it was just something he did, AC/DC man started humming The Beach Boys' old tune 'Help Me, Rhonda'. Although when he started singing it as the swab wandered around my mouth, he had his own words.

'Got the Rona, got, got the Rona.

Got the Rona, yeah, coughin' up my lungs.'

The nurse said, 'You're the third person he's serenaded today.' And he smiled a little as we finished the test.

There was a pause and then I nodded. 'Good day for it.'

•

I spent the rest of the rehearsal on Zoom.

Zoom sounds like it is something that could be a whole lot of things. A sideshow alley ride at the Royal Brisbane Show that you thought was the best thing ever. Maybe an ice-cream or chewy you might enjoy as you walked home from school. Or some lame-arsed party drug you took at a lame-arsed party at uni. Zoom could be a form of cleaning product – maybe a bleach that a ning-nong or an American president might take if they had Covid.

As it was, Zoom managed to sprout a squadron of words from the manner of Zooming your way through meetings, social catch-ups and work conferences; it led to the inadvertent entrances and exits of family members, pets and the occasional tradie or delivery worker – Zoom-bombing, in other words.

And the two sisters who played Corona Lotto and shared a 'vino quarantino' had to have a stiff 'quarantini' (cocktail) or two with another friend who had been zumped: dumped over Zoom during virtual happy hour.

I enjoyed Zoom rehearsals more than I could ever have imagined. People still banged on a lot, and some parts were a bit creaky, but the work was pretty good. With a bit of distance, I realised how good the play was. And how good the rest of the cast was, how adept and kind the director was and how good the set was.

It was an iso lesson. Sometimes a bit of perspective makes you see something you were missing when you didn't take the time to look properly. Or, in other words, get your head out of your arse and actually see what's happening and what's good.

Or maybe it was because I had taken up the quite lovely pastime of indulging in the odd Jaffa or two.

For Jaffas fix everything.

CHAPTER 4
A STITCH IN TIME

I stood in front of a display at the Albany Whaling Museum and concentrated on the image in front of me because I felt a bit embarrassed to look at the view that had caught my eye. An oldish bloke, a retired marine engineer, had bent over to pick up a bit of rubbish and that was the view. Him bending over.

I knew the old bloke was a marine engineer because he'd told me and everybody else, especially the tour guide, whom he had been correcting on quite a few facts as we had wandered around. Facts like the performance of some of the vessels in the museum, the equipment in the museum and even weather events mentioned by the guide. At one point the old man took a small notebook from his trousers to check a fact.

The Albany whaling station at the bottom of Western Australia stopped operating in 1978. That was when the last whale-chasers prowled into the docks next to the station. The ships were dressed up for the day in bunting and flying flags, wearing their best for the last waltz. The industry and the jobs were gone. The masters let every crew member pull a trigger on the harpoon cannon, just so they had a story to tell. They had headed out in anger on that last day, but, in the words of the town's mayor who had tried to save the station and was given the honour of being a crewman for the day in recognition of his efforts, 'We didn't see a bloody whale all day.'

On the way back, after a harpoon was shot in the direction of the now obsolete station as one last defiant gesture, one of the skippers relaxed the no alcohol restrictions and broke out the beers.

'Get stuck in, boys, what are they going to do? Sack us?'

There are photos of the whalers on the decks getting, as the skipper ordered, stuck in. They are dressed in gear, or clobber as my father would have called the clothes the men wore, that could only be worn by Australians.

Whaling makes me think of Herman Melville's sailors of nineteenth-century Nantucket, Captain Ahab and his crew on the *Pequod*. Or, more accurately, some creaking old film version of the book – which was actually pretty good when you got past all the 'ooo' and 'rrrrrr' sailor acting.

It was sometimes the Sunday matinee on a rainy arvo and I'd watch it with my parents and siblings. My mum liked it because she liked Gregory Peck, who played Ahab. 'Not as handsome as he was in *The Keys of the Kingdom*. A good-looking lad in a priest's gear. Lovely.'

'He's wearing no dog collar.'

'What?' said my mother, as a surly Gregory Peck clumped around on his wooden leg.

'Gregory Peck isn't a priest in this one.'

'Of course he's not.'

'He's a bit wooden in this, isn't he?' said my father. A pause. 'Wooden as his wooden leg.'

'Oh, shut your trap,' said my mum, and it was said in the way someone else might say, 'I love you.'

Of course he didn't.

'He looks as useful as a Redcliffe winger with that gammy leg of his.'

'Oh, be quiet.'

Nobody was quiet, and any remaining existentialist drama from Old Herman's original work was lost in the banter.

Gregory Peck did a lot of yelling. When he bellowed, 'HE BREACHES!' as Moby-Dick shot to the surface, my mother said he sounded like he'd just missed a bus to Sandgate Station. And when Ahab, driven by his desire to kill Moby-Dick, exhorts his men to row faster and then cries out, 'There! Do you see the white whale, men?'

There was a pause and then my father's rather incredulous tone. 'Why's he asking if they can see the whale? All the poor buggers are facing him as they row. They turn around to the big fish finger, they'll bugger the stroke. What a yobbo. Typical officer.'

'Yobbo Ahab,' said my mum. 'Sounds more like a Danish architect than a whaler.' As a result, *Moby Dick* became the movie where Gregory Peck played the Danish architect with the wooden leg, who was looking for an opera house to design.

Whaling also meant Japanese crewmen in their blue overalls and white safety helmets, firing water cannons at anti-whaling demonstrators from Greenpeace or Sea Shepherd or some such organisation. I remember seeing that footage on a television documentary in a lounge room of a house in Perth.

Families liked watching television together in those days.

One of the daughters was going out with me, so I was invited to dinner with the family, and after dinner we watched television. That's where I saw the whalers, and I heard the father laugh. 'Look at them. Japanese do love uniforms, don't they?'

On the wall of that home were photos of the family. The three daughters as children, one of the mother in her wedding dress holding her new husband's arm and quite a few of the father. With the exception of the black formal wedding suit he wore, all the photos were of him in white lab coats. He was a pharmacist. He liked his uniforms. They told people what he did. And yet he had a little laugh at the Japanese, because they liked their uniforms.

And now whaling meant the men of Albany. The men whose photos were plastered on displays throughout the museum. Blokes wearing clobber that only Australian whalers would wear. I wouldn't fancy Moby-Dick's chances against them, or Greenpeace or Sea Shepherd's for that matter. The men were just lolling about, but there was an implied hardness in even the idea of what they were capable of, with their flensing knives. On that last trip into home, they lounged on the decks, getting stuck in, sucking on stubbies of Emu Bitter.

Some wore the ageless uniform of the practical bloke in winter. A woollen cap known as a beanie (because of the bean-sized button that used to rest at the crown of the cap). In some parts of regional Australia it is known as a 'scone warmer' and within my own family as a 'brain cuddler'.

I looked at the images. It must have been winter.

I have a friend who has a simple theory about when you can tell it's winter in Queensland: the couch is dormant. By this he means, once the thermometer drops below the temperature at which Queensland couch grass will grow (roughly 25 degrees Celsius, according to my friend's bog-standard gardening knowledge), Queensland is officially in winter.

One mustn't be too prescriptive about things and a sense of perspective can help because winter is usually the time people break out in moans about the cold mornings and nights so perhaps we Queenslanders should try to think of how The Unfortunates feel about our dormant couch winters.

The Unfortunates are Southerners, souls who live in Sydney and Melbourne where a Queensland winter day of a low 20 degrees Celsius would be welcomed as a blessing from above. It'd be enough to have them wearing t-shirts, thongs and singing Billy Thorpe's 'It's Almost Summer' to themselves.

But we'll leave them where they are and deal with a Queensland winter. Those months of crisp clear days, where the roof seems to have been lifted off the landscape, such is the glory of Brisbane winter light. It's the spouts and splashes of breeching whales as they migrate up the coast and it's a time not for harpoons, but for jumpers.

I love jumpers and their daggy cousin, the cardigan. I always felt, even as a kid, when you got a jumper out of a closet and whacked it on, it was a bit of a deal. Add a brain cuddler and you were off on a climate adventure.

This is where the selection of winter clothes can be problematical, because in my humble boofheaded opinion when it comes to winter wear, less is more. Too often, people think winter is an excuse to break out outfits that not even Sir Douglas Mawson would have thought to wear on an Antarctic expedition. Things like puffer jackets, a nylon or polyester creation stuffed with duck or goose down, which is overkill. Now on the winter streets of Melbourne, or in the harsher climes of the Northern Hemisphere, these things can be invaluable, but walking around Queensland in these rather ugly garments is just asking to turn yourself into a steamed dim sum.

They make people look like the Michelin Man and they rustle like a collection of old-fashioned plastic shopping bags when you walk.

Polar fleece? Okay, but I can't go past a jumper or cardie. I used to like woollen vests but I've since decided they are slightly attention-seeking and eccentric, a little like wearing bow ties instead of neckties.

The great thing about cardigans is that they almost always have lovely deep pockets which can be a bit like Dr Who's Tardis, with its elastic internal dimensions.

I worked with a director once who was mad for cardies and what that man could pull out and put in his cardigan pockets wasn't to be believed. He would have put Mandrake the Magician and his top hat to shame.

Jumpers and cardigans are always at their peak when made of natural fibre. Not only is it breathable but it is also elastic, which is not to be sniffed at if you have been in a good paddock. You try and squeeze yourself into a synthetic jumper and you'll end up looking like you have a Galapagos tortoise sleeping on your stomach.

And you can keep jumpers for yonks, for they age like fine wine. Some may say you can't hang on to a beloved woolly jumper past its use-by date but I say that's when you start to get a bit of character in your wardrobe.

I consider some old football jerseys to be a member of the jumper family and my white-shouldered long-sleeved maroon Redcliffe Dolphins jersey is perfect for a dormant couch winter outing.

In Paris, I was going about my business, mooching along, taking in the sights, when I was asked by an Australian voice to move. The voice belonged to a woman trying to take a photo of the Notre Dame Cathedral. Apparently, I was ruining her shot.

As this woman was at least twenty metres away from me I didn't quite understand her point. I looked at her and she sighed, saying, 'I don't mean to be rude but you're wearing a Brothers footy jersey and you look like a transplanted Moreton Bay fig. I don't mind Brothers but I'm from Redlands and you just scream Brisbane. I'm just after a shot of the cathedral.'

Fair enough. I nodded and moved to one side.

I didn't see any footy jerseys among the whalers. I was surprised. But then what they did was dirty work; why ruin something as wonderful as a footy jersey? Most were dressed in blue singlets, footy shorts or jeans. And on their feet, of all things, were thongs. At a pinch I could imagine Queequeg wearing thongs on the *Pequod*, but he would have called them jandals I suppose, being a Kiwi. Well, at least he was supposed to be one in the film.

The blue singlets are interesting. An English actor I did a play with asked me why on earth, 'You Australians call an undershirt a singlet? It's bad enough having the Yanks call them vests.'

I said that it made sense to me to call the thing a singlet because that's what I had always called it. 'Try getting a hold of what something is called when they are also known as a Jackie Howe or a wife-beater.'

This lost the Pommy actor.

'What? Jackie Howe? That sounds like some cabaret singer, like . . . like a Shirley Bassey or Cilla Black.'

The idea of Shirley Bassey wearing a blue singlet while singing 'Goldfinger' made me laugh. I explained that Jackie Howe was a shearer who broke a world record for shearing rams while wearing a blue singlet – sorry, undershirt. It gave Jackie more freedom to move his arms and grapple with the sheep than a regular cotton shirt did. 'There's even a statue of him somewhere,' I said.

'Of an undershirt? A statue of an undershirt?'

'No, of Jackie Howe.'

The English actor tapped on his phone as we sat in our dressing room. The tapping stopped. The English actor had come up with an image of the statue online. There on his screen stood a pretty well-groomed Jackie holding a ram against his chest in his chiselled arms.

'Christ. Are you sure Jackie isn't a New Zealander? Look what he's doing with the sheep! And he's smiling.'

'He's grimacing,' I said.

The English actor shot me a look that made me laugh.

On reflection, the statue of Jackie did look pretty satisfied with itself, so maybe it was a grimace-cum-smirk. More smirk than grimace, at best.

'One man's grimace is another man's smile,' said the English actor.

We both laughed.

'God, that's an awful thing to say.' And after a moment he said without humour, 'And so is calling it a wife-beater.'

He was right.

•

My parents' generation called singlets Jackie Howes and my father wore them on house-building jobs under a shirt. When the work started, off went the shirt, and when the work stopped, on went the shirt. Even for lunch or 'smoko'. (Smoko came from the idea of having a break to have a smoke and then gradually took over as an all-encompassing term for any type of break. If workers had cigarettes back then they'd have a roll-your-own or if it was a tailor-made then it'd be a diminutive: a Styvo (Peter Stuyvesant), a BH (Benson & Hedges) or a Winnie Red or a Winnie Blue (Winfield) – or they'd just say it was a dart, a durry, a coffin nail or a gasper, or at least a ciggie, but heaven forbid that you called it a cigarette.)

A Jackie Howe became a working man's uniform, along with shorts and a carpentry belt with a hammer slung at the side.

If my old man was going to do something around the yard of a weekend, he'd take off his 'good' clothes, usually a moth-eaten or torn t-shirt, and throw on 'a Jackie'.

Woodchoppers at the Royal Shows would wear white singlets, but it was always the blue singlets that were associated with doing something useful rather than just doing something to impress.

Once my mother had delegated my old man to go and chop wood for the fire and he was none too quick about it. She stuck her head out the back door and told him to 'Make more like a woodchopper at the Ekka [Royal Queensland Show, originally called the Brisbane Exhibition] than someone solving the world's woes.' My old man smiled and nodded. Then he bent down and picked up a block to chop, looked at it for a long moment and bent down further. He lay his finger on the block and then rose up and held out his finger to me. On it was a Christmas beetle. A golden-winged scarab that slowly crawled on my father's finger, and then stood still. He held it for a long time. Then the thing gathered itself and flew off, shining briefly in the sunlight.

'The things you find when you take your time,' my father said. 'Christmas is coming.' He picked up the axe slowly.

'Chopping a block of wood in quick time is something to boast about,' he told me, 'but really all you've done is bugger all and three parts of useless. But definitely impressive.' He looked up at the sky, the sun was going down and a great golden and orange glow flooded above. 'Slow and steady is the go on an arvo like this. Least we can appreciate the show that's going on up there.'

His big arms and shoulders swung slowly but with a steady power and I stood around pretending to put bits of wood in a barrow. He seemed immense.

He whistled a song. 'It's a Lovely Day Tomorrow'. He took his time and the sun set and we enjoyed the show it put on.

How a singlet became known as a 'wife-beater' is a little unclear, it could just be basic snobbery that a working man who wears a blue singlet would be more likely to belt 'the missus' (the man's wife or Mrs; a piece of Cockney slang that made the journey to Australia with colonisation) after having a few after-work beers. Short-tempered and unable to deal with life. The idea that only a certain type of man from a certain type of demographic was capable of such acts was a lie.

A wardrobe designer once told me that they were called wife-beaters because a man who beat his wife to death in America after World War II was pictured being arrested in a white singlet splattered with the poor victim's blood. His picture was published in the paper with the headline, 'Wife Beater Arrested'.

The designer said that images of thuggish men from popular culture, like Marlon Brando's performance as Stanley Kowalski in *A Streetcar Named Desire*, only popularised the image because it was wrapped up in a charismatic performer and allowed people's preconceptions and assumptions to be reinforced.

My old man mightn't have been Marlon Brando, he mightn't have been a theatrical legend and cultural icon, but then he didn't have any interest in being that. He was a bloke who wore his Jackie Howe when he worked and when he whistled a sweet tune. When he told me to look above to see the show the sunset put on, when he held out a golden sign that Christmas was on the way. He was a man who loved his wife and never touched any of his family in anger.

I looked at the Albany whalers in the photos. They might have looked like they were hard and capable of doing something awful, because, quite frankly, the job of gutting and cleaning and flensing a whale was an awful business, but it was just a job.

I thought of the mother from the airport, how her hand had gently touched the head of her child as news of an unspeakable, wretched act of domestic violence was played on a television screen. It didn't seem that funny at all to call a blue singlet a wife-beater, as if domestic violence was so common and so accepted to be the basis of a joke. A joke about a piece of clothing that good men like my father wore.

•

And why would people pay attention to actors? Even great ones like Marlon Brando.

Marlon Brando himself put it best when asked in some interview, 'What actually is an actor?'

'An actor?' he said. 'What's an actor? He's a man who if you ain't talking about him, he ain't listening.'

I have seen actors trying to 'macho' or 'bloke up' their image by wearing a Jackie Howe. To try to look the part of a bloke who could break a world-shearing record with a smile or a grimace on his face, or somebody that could channel an inner Brando. And I've seen those actors come a real gutser.

During the very play where the English actor was complaining why an undershirt was called a singlet, and after a weekend where *A Streetcar Named Desire* was screened with an accompanying documentary, another cast member suddenly appeared in a blue singlet. The play was set in Restoration England and, as he was playing a dandified fop in the production, the singlet seemed at strange odds with what the play called for. The director, who was a kind and generous man, said nothing but pursed his lips and tilted his head to one side.

The actor in the blue singlet was very slight and somehow made what he was wearing look like a voluminous nightshirt as he 'fopped' around the court intrigue of some English king. The English actor whispered to me, 'Hello, here's Wee Willie Winkie.'

Wee Willie Winkie was some bloke from an old nursery rhyme who ran through town in his nightgown.

It was hard not to laugh.

Then a polite voice, the director: 'Just hold it there, please.'

There was an agonising pause. The director again, this time in an almost pitying yet truly bewildered tone.

'Why?'

He looked at Wee Willie Winkie.

It was very hard not to giggle.

The pause extended.

'I just thought I would play around, try to bring an implied violence.'

Another pause.

'To the – well, try to find it, perhaps, in the part.'

There was an even more agonised quiet. And then a kind voice said, 'Really, it's so implied as to be less than slight. In fact it's not there. Don't go looking for something that simply doesn't exist.'

The first person to laugh was Wee Willie Winkie himself and, as he went and put on a frock shirt, another cast member swore they heard the director mutter, 'Bloody Marlon Brando has a lot to answer for.'

•

I laughed and looked at the Albany Whalers and thought of Wee Willie Winkie on the harpoon. There was a lot to take from those photos in the museum and I thought it vaguely interesting that work clothes had been adapted away from practicality into fashion wear.

Not long before, I'd gone off to find a new pair of garden clogs, some bowdlerised version of the much-unloved and loathed Croc footwear. My Croc crimes list is as long as a rainy long weekend and, even though I am a rusted-on adherent of this by-product of the petrochemical industry, I have never been ignorant of the fact that the things are bloody ugly. Garden Crocs are some American cousin and are lovely to wear while one bumbles about in the garden picking up dog poo. They are also handy when placed by the front door to don for a quick dash across the front lawn to put the bins out for collection early in the morning when you hear the rubbish trucks gasping and creaking along the street.

There was an old-school hardware shop in my neighbourhood, a proper one that sold things people on the land needed – proper tools, proper hoses, proper barrows that looked sturdy and solid, like something out of a 'Made in Australia' documentary from the Department of Industry. Not a hint of Bunnings about it and the only nod to the demographic of where I lived, a sniff of the gentrification, was a well-presented rack of garden clogs, called Sloggers.

What occurred to me on that morning I went looking for a new pair of Sloggers will happen to everybody sooner or later: that moment of having something in your life that you have grown used to suddenly disappear.

Like one of the drivers from the classic French film *The Wages of Fear*, a dramatisation about a misfit group of workers who drive in a convoy carrying a deadly cargo of explosives:

one by one they meet their end before they can get their reward. One, who seemed the toughest, sits in the cabin with his co-driver, slipping in and out of consciousness. He's on the brink of death and the driver urges him to keep talking.

Where did he live in Paris?

The tough driver tells of a long street with a long white fence.

The driver says he remembers the fence.

'What lies beyond the fence?' asks the driver.

The tough man says nothing. He closes his eyes. And after a pause he opens them slowly and mutters, 'What lies beyond.' His eyes go wide, and he says suddenly, 'Nothing!'

And he dies.

If you're going to have a French existentialist moment, there you go.

That's what happened when I went to get my Sloggers.

Nothing!

The proper rural hardware shop had gone. It was like it had never been there. In its place was a homewares store, with some of the same expensive items that the coffee shop general stores had on the beach. The old shop had been gutted, peeled of all its character and flesh, like a whale on the flensing decks in Albany. Well and truly renovated beyond all recognition. The only thing that even hinted at the shop's former incarnation was an intricate shelf of small compartments for screws and bolts, each with a neatly handwritten figure to indicate the size of the items held in the small drawers.

It was a startling shock and I felt slightly out of kilter.

A very nice woman must have seen me looking at the last trace of the proper hardware shop, the drawer compartments. She came up and said, 'You're looking for some machinery, aren't you? This is all that's left of the hardware shop, I'm afraid, but it is such a beautiful feature, a real talking point.'

A part of me was pleased that she thought a ponce like me looked capable enough of wanting such equipment.

I admitted I was after Sloggers.

'Oh,' she exclaimed, delighted that I was one of the poncy tribes who liked nice things and not a practical man on the land. 'We're going to get those back in but that'll take a while. Who would have thought something so ugly would be fashionable? Well, I shouldn't call them ugly, they're just sensible. We do have boots though.'

She showed me a selection of things that I took to be gumboots. They all had patterns on them. Like some Laura Ashley nightmares from the 1980s.

She looked at me.

'They really aren't you, are they?'

I admitted they weren't.

I saw they were called Wellington boots. My aunt, who was Welsh and a dairy farmer, always called them that or 'my wellies' and never gumboots.

I looked down and said slowly, 'What's the difference between wellies and gumboots?'

'About thirty dollars,' the woman said. And then she laughed. 'We've actually got some gumboots here.' And she held up a pair of boots that looked like they were covered in a Ken Done knock-off. What, I wondered, was the fascination with boots and bad '80s patterns?

The woman held up a Ken Done and a Laura Ashley boot. She raised the Laura Ashley, 'This is a Wellington boot, and they are a bit more sculpted, bit comfier than a gumboot.' She held out a Ken Done so I could see. 'That's the difference between them.'

I looked at them and then at her.

'The Wellington boots are based around riding boots that the Duke of Wellington wore when he was giving Napoleon what for, and the gumboots are called gumboots because they are made from rubber gum. Good old literal Aussie diminutives at work. Good pair of gummies for you.'

I nodded. I was going to ask her how she knew all of that, but she smiled.

'Retired history teacher!' she said as an explanation.

I asked if they had any plain gumboots and she laughed. 'Not that sort of a shop anymore I'm afraid.'

I couldn't see the difference in the boots that clearly, but the more I looked, I could see the wellies were tapered at the top and had different material there as well, which would have led to a snugger fit.

But I seriously doubted that the Duke of Wellington would have worn a floral Wellington boot as he was busy giving Napoleon what for.

I found myself wondering about 'Good old literal Aussie diminutives'. Here in front of me, wrapped in Ken Done prints, was the evidence. 'Boots made from rubber tree gum' became gumboots.

As if on cue, a couple of other shoppers came in and asked if there were more of those 'comfy cossies', in the same colour they'd bought the other day. The pleasant retired teacher walked over to a rack and held up two one-piece bathing suits, aka togs if you are from Queensland, bathers if you're from anywhere else in Australia, or swimming costumes. Cossies. Comfortable becomes comfy.

'Thought you might come back after the barbie,' said the retired history teacher.

'Beauty!' one of the shoppers said.

I don't know why Australians shorten words and have a tendency to put an 'ie' sound on the back end of the diminutive, but I am glad they do. I laughed a little.

The retired teacher looked over. 'You're not tempted to get a pair, are you? The wellies won't be in your size, but the gumboots might be.'

I couldn't help myself and asked the retired history teacher, 'Do you have any nighties? As in Wee Willie Winkie?'

'Oh my god.' She laughed. 'To think I thought you were after a farm tool!' She shook her head and said, 'I have some nice PJs though.'

I nodded and said, pointing to the boots, 'I was tempted, but I'll wait for the Sloggers.'

She gave me a thumbs-up. 'Just give us a tingle in about a month.' And she went on chatting to the other shoppers.

•

Work clobber as fashion. It happens. Dungarees or jeans were hardy cotton trousers that were worn by various manual workers like miners, cattle workers, farmers and factory workers before they were transformed into a rebellious statement – think James Dean and our old mate Marlon Brando.

I looked at the Albany whalers. There was a lot of footy short action on the decks. That's what footy shorts were for – engaging in physical activity, giving freedom of movement, and that almost mythical, though incorrect, claim of 'one size fits all'.

Footy shorts are for footy, be they the Rolls Royce of the species – rugby union Ruggers – or the more questionable rugby league shorts, which are like wearing shopping bags. Australian rules shorts were the shortest of the codes, and soccer shorts by far the baggiest.

For work and labour, footy shorts are maybe fine. As a piece of fashion wear? Never. Articles of clothing which are known by such endearing nicknames as 'outer nut sack', 'balls divider', and the graphic 'nut-splitters' should never be worn to a social occasion.

Tell that to a younger version of myself, who for some reason thought that a pair of nut splitters, a body shirt and thongs were the ideal outfit to wear to an engagement party.

In my defence, I thought it was simply a barbecue. Perhaps I hadn't listened properly, and it wasn't until I saw the face of the girl who'd invited me that I realised I had seriously misread the situation.

An older gent, who later turned out to be an uncle of the intended bride, thought I had come to spike the keg.

He took my mauve body shirt to be a barman's outfit and the footy shorts as a sign that I was also doing cellar duty.

As for the bride's mother, she sidled up to her niece – who had invited me – and asked if I spoke much English because she thought I was a New Australian. 'The tall lad wearing the European-type clothes, you know the sort that they take off in an instant to go swimming. They're like that, you know.'

When she came up and spoke to me, she did so slowly and very loudly, for I couldn't have very much English considering the way I was dressed. Apparently shouting every syllable slowly makes English more understandable. 'Where . . . ARE . . . YOU . . . FROM?' she bellowed, pointing her finger at me.

'Redcliffe,' I said.

She was still and then a look crossed her face as if she should go off and lock the drawer with the good cutlery in it.

I didn't get an invite to the wedding.

Trying to make the quantum leap from workwear to tailored trousers was a leap too.

Let me explain.

In the afternoons of my youth there was a plethora of television shows where a young protagonist, nearly always a boy, would somehow befriend some half-wild animal and have various adventures, all overseen by a dad.

All that was required of the dad, who was almost always practical and capable with a firm jaw and tidy hair, was to be stern in a kind way and be able to grin on command. He usually had some job like a ranger or charter boat operator or any such low-level adventurer occupation.

If there was a mother involved in these shows, she was lucky if she made it out of the kitchen and then it would only be as far as the verandah, where she could gaze off into the distance and maybe glimpse the action.

They were all the same shows really: *Flipper*, about a dolphin; *Lassie*, about a dog; and *Gentle Ben*, about a bear. The last one had the best opening credits where the kid, the bear and the dad roared across the Everglades in a boat with a great big propeller. The bear was chained to the boat and was apparently medicated with tranquilisers within an inch of its life for the filming, but still the square-jawed dad looked slightly leery of the whole thing.

The Australian version of these shows, *Skippy the Bush Kangaroo*, had a dad called Matt Hammond who was a ranger in a national park. He was the most realistic of all the TV pretend fathers because he wasn't above being grumpy and shouting. In fact, old Matt Hammond would shout at everybody – his shadow, his middle son, his youngest who was the kangaroo's best friend, the helicopter pilot Jerry, and even the kangaroo.

And I kind of liked him because of it.

It was a rare thing to hear fathers shouting in these shows and perhaps that was why my own father was quite fond of *Skippy* as well. He used to call Matt Hammond 'Old Accordion Daks' because the trousers Matt wore were chronically crinkled around the crotch area. This was, I hasten to add, caused by all the times a TV father has to get up and sit down from a desk, or get in and out of a car, which seemed to be the prerequisite action involved in being a TV patriarchal figure. And all the shouting he had to do, and Matt did a lot, as well as run around Waratah National Park.

'Come on, Acco Daks,' I remember my old man saying as Matt was about to yell at Jerry. 'Give it to him with both barrels.'

Acco Daks had morphed from Accordion Trousers and could also be termed Action Daks, and came to mean active pants. Theoretically one could refer to activewear – the tight-fitting Lycra-based fitness outfits which seem to be worn by its adherents to almost any conceivable location – as modern-day Acco Daks.

But true Acco Daks have to have Accordion Crotch. And the curse of Accordion Crotch was never a good look, even if it was honestly earned. I was gormless enough to ask my mother if you could iron Accordion Crotch out.

'Well, there's a thought, dear, why don't you get a pair of your father's shorts and give it a go.'

'Don't be touching my daks, Sunshine. Sisyphus would have more luck with his stone ball than anybody flattening out the accordion.'

I just stared. Greek legend meets the accordion.

'Very hard to get them out, natural fibre, that's why your father prefers his safari suit,' my mother said airily.

My father laughed. 'Come off it, I've worn that bag of fruit twice. Terrible bloody thing.' He was referring to a polyester safari suit that he had bought at half price off a customer who had come across this example of unique 'non-iron miracle clothes' that had fallen off the back of a truck.

The only Accordion Crotch–free fabrics were synthetic, perhaps one of the '-ons', rayon or nylon. Or their cousin, polyester.

This didn't stop Efco, makers of the legendary Acco Daks shorts – Stubbies – from having a crack at creating a pair of dress strides based on workwear. They even had the temerity to call them Strides.

A mate called Mark Hunt, or Marconi as he was known to his friends, was associated professionally with Strides, garments he called the Leyland P-76 of trousers. Mark went by the name Marconi after a relief teacher took an economics lesson when the regular teacher was ill. The relief teacher went through the roll and called out each boy's name methodically and loudly. When he came to Mark Hunt, he repeated the name, and it hung in the air. Mark always let his name be called three time by relief teachers. It had a similar effect to the old stitch-up of getting someone to say 'Mike Hunt' over and over again. The relief teacher was obviously an old hand and stopped saying Mark Hunt mid-pronunciation and turned it, for whatever reason, into Marconi.

The name stuck.

Mostly because Mark's communication style was a little like the first broadcasts of Marconi's wireless — scrambly and hard to decipher.

Marconi (Mark, not the inventor) had a part-time job at a menswear shop called Miser Jones and it was here he sold the dreaded Strides. 'Couldn't believe how many pairs we sold the first couple of weeks. Strides were walking out the door.'

Apparently, they came back in the hands of unhappy customers. Strides may have been wrinkle-free but they were also close to unwearable.

'It was the crotch. Or lack of. No room, not even for a pair of marbles, especially if you were wearing undies. The only blokes who could wear them comfortably were the Thunderbirds because they had no tackle to show and didn't need to wear grundies. Just like the kids from the country.'

Why people from the country were likely not to wear underdaks is based around the snobbish generalisations that such folk were a bit less down the evolutionary path than people in the city and were probably too poor to afford such luxury items anyway.

Marconi was also implying the marionettes from International Rescue, the Thunderbirds, went undie-less. Or went commando. Or free-balled. It was insane to suggest that puppets would wear grundies in the first place, but one must enjoy Australians' continued enjoyment and adherence to rhyming slang. Reg Grundy. A television pioneer in Australia who was at times a radio DJ, then television gameshow host, then a television gameshow producer, then a producer of drama, then a corporate mogul who lived a long and very happy life. A Reg Grundy Production became a Grundy's Production and whoever made the connection between undies and Grundy's cracked a sociolinguistics jackpot.

I wonder if Reg ever thought that perhaps his greatest legacy was to have his name added to the Australian lexicon as a piece of intimate apparel. I'd like to think so.

And I would have loved to have known his reaction to a wondrous piece of fatherly advice to a son I overheard when I went on a fishing trip with a school mate. Of course it was Marconi, who had to run to the toilet to do number twos while his father was hitching the tinnie runabout to their family car.

As Marconi trotted across the carpark to the toilet block, his dad yelled in that frustrated father way, no doubt deep in his anger at having to put up with two idiot boys and his embarrassment in not being capable of getting the trailer hitch over the towing ball: 'Mark! Make sure you wipe your bum properly. Your mother's sick of Reg Grundies with more skid marks than Peter Brock's driveway.'

Skid marks, known in our family as Richard Widmarks (rhyming slang again, this time using Richard Widmark, a popular American actor from the Western films my mum liked), need no explanation. They were talked about once by a sports master who was trying to drum some higher life goal into us students on a rainy morning. 'You've got to make your mark in life, and skid marks on your undies don't count.'

Inspiring stuff: the Redcliffe version of *'Carpe diem'* from *Dead Poets Society*.

•

Back to the Albany Whaling Museum. And the retired marine engineer. And the view I had seen.

The retired marine engineer was definitely wearing Acco Daks, the reviled cargo pants. He was obviously a man who liked to take his utensils with him wherever he went. His pockets bulged with items as diverse as a torch, a wallet, extra socks, sunblock, a giggle hat, keys, notebooks, cameras and a phone. And biscuits. Choc-covered digestives.

I'd seen him and his partner around the museum before the tour began and he was constantly emptying and repacking his pockets in search of whatever it was he needed. He and his partner had sat on a bench having a coffee and then the thought must have struck him that a digestive would go well with the coffee. Up he got, emptied his pockets, found the digestives, popped out a few on the bench, repacked his pockets, forgot something. Took a time to find whatever it was that he was looking for, which turned out to be a small sachet of sugar he must have nicked from some coffee shop, and then repacked his pockets and sat down. On his digestive.

He must have brushed it somehow, for he sat on it choc-side up.

And when he got up and walked off, the digestive was riveted to his Acco Daks. Seagulls followed in his wake as if he were some great ship churning up titbits from the waves.

When the digestive lost its grip and fell to the ground it was quickly demolished by the gulls and, to quote the sports master, it looked like he had made his mark in life.

So many euphemisms came floating to me from the past. Arse-rust, nugget print and quoit rivet, all of which I had heard in various sporting change rooms. And one from a wardrobe assistant from a television series, who echoed Marconi's mum when she said she was over all the 'organic prints' left by a particular cast member on their costume.

The retired marine engineer hadn't seen his digestive print, and I wondered if anyone else had. Did it matter?

Knowing it wasn't what it looked like didn't help. It was embarrassing and funny, but I suppose it was just life.

As any of those whalers in the photos throughout the museum would tell you, worse things happen at sea.

CHAPTER 5
SPORTING TIMES

Walking the dog one Saturday morning, I came across a little collection of people engaging in a ritual that would be repeated right across the nation in one form or another that day, almost an act of communion. Saturday morning sport. In this case, footy. Australian rules. And I had come just in time to hear the homily from the coach. A little pep talk. The kids jiggling about in front of him.

They would have been about ten, a truly beautiful age for a human being when they are just beginning to grow into their bodies, the leaping-off point for the journey to the sort of people they'll become, but they are still little enough to be kids. And that meant they were paying attention to everything except what the coach was trying to say.

'Focus! Come on, focus!' he said.

The coach was on a hiding to nothing, even though he was doing his best to try to inspire and guide. He must have been one of the kids' dads, because that is nearly always the case with kids' sports, some poor parent who knows a little about the sport is volunteered to the role. And he was holding his coffee in a keep cup with 'DAD' written on it in a child's writing. He swirled the cup as if it were a sign for the team to assemble.

'Focus, guys. Time for game faces!'

A couple of kids pulled ridiculous eye-popping faces and then they fell about in peals of laughter. One little boy focused on what he was picking from his nose. Another was intently studying a stem of grass and wafting it to and fro as if it were a magic wand. Another with her hair in a tight bun on top of her head was trying to hit the top of the hand of a teammate who was trying to pull it away before contact was made. Not quick enough.

There was a slap. A scream. More peals of laughter from the two hand-slappers.

The bloke with the keep cup said, 'Hayley, don't hit so hard.'

'Yes, Daddy.'

He winced a little. 'Coach, call me Coach.'

'Okay, Coach Daddy.'

He tried not to laugh, but the parents behind him didn't help. They giggled and so Coach took a deep breath and offered some advice, a collection of hoary old chestnuts that coaches have uttered since time began. Just so he could feel like a coach.

He pointed out that to be a good team, 'We have to look like a team! Tuck your shirts in and pull your socks up!'

'Why?' asked the boy with the grass.

'To run faster. It makes you run faster.'

The kid with the grass gave a suitably sceptical look that made the coach almost laugh.

'It's a known fact, Ryan.'

Ryan wafted his grassy magic wand.

The boy who was picking his nose said, rather absent-mindedly as he looked over at the opposition, 'They're big.'

I thought to myself, Don't say it, Coach, but of course he did.

'They're not that big.'

The kid stopped picking his nose, although he left his finger in his nostril and gave the coach a look.

Being told by a grown-up, 'They're not that big,' gives a kid no comfort because the first thing they think is, 'Maybe not to you, you're a grown-up!'

The coach raised his coffee in salute and resignation. 'Off you go, get out there and enjoy yourselves!'

'Inspiring stuff, Coach Daddy,' said one of the parents.

'Here to help,' said Coach Daddy and they all smiled a little. And he sipped from his Coach Daddy keep cup.

With socks pulled high, shirts tucked in and Ryan wafting his wand, the kids shambled out to play.

I walked on with the dog, thinking. Sport. We're told, incessantly, that Australians love it. Love playing and love watching it. A good friend of mine insists that isn't true, that it is just shoved down our collective throats like we're beasts in a feeding lot being force-fed before slaughter. I think she's a nice person with a greenish hue who lays it on a bit thick. She thinks I'm a member of COFA.

Whether her idea is true or not, sport and the relationship we have with it have opened up a whole universe of language that goes right across the social spectrum.

Take politics. Politicians love a sporty phrase. John Howard basically dropped a seed of doubt that grew into a full-blown tree that was partly to blame for one of the most qualified people to be prime minister never to be prime minister. John Howard said of Kim Beazley, the affable and gifted Labor leader, that he was a good bloke but he 'didn't have the ticker' to be an effective leader.

The ticker. Old-school Australian for the heart. The heart beats along like a timepiece. It becomes a ticker. And the heart defines your character. Someone 'has a big heart'. You can be a flashy player, have a load of talent, but you won't amount to much without 'ticker'.

It always amused me that John Howard could play the sport card so effectively, the way he walked around each morning in a collection of national team tracksuits and the way he could field off his own bowling. His infamous attempt to play cricket with the locals while visiting Pakistan ended up with his attempt to bowl a ball almost hitting his own feet.

But he was also a smart and cunning political operator, so well played him. It seemed to work for quite a while.

In many ways sport is the great family photo album of slang. You open it up and there are all the old-timers, only in this album they still get out amongst the language. It is madness to hear a young footballer born this century praise a teammate as having 'a heart as big as Phar Lap's'.

Some might call handing down a bit of slang the passing of tradition through the generations, but I would love for an interviewer to ask one of those players who or what Phar Lap was, and even how Phar Lap is spelt. If anyone says a New Zealand–born gelding that stood seventeen hands high and that the name is Thai for lightning, I would be surprised. I was told that by a Mr Errol Exeter, one of the first rugby coaches I had, when he tried to explain why being likened to an internal horse organ was a good thing.

Another boy asked why it couldn't be an Australian horse that had a big heart and Mr Exeter said that Phar Lap was an Australian horse.

'How?' asked the boy.

'ANZACs,' said Mr Exeter, 'Australian and New Zealand Army Corps. If the Kiwis were good enough to shed blood alongside our boys at Gallipoli, then they are good enough to be Australians.' He paused and then added, 'Whenever we want them to be.'

Australian prime ministers don't just use sporting slang, sometimes they *are* the slang. How many young players would know that an affable, uninspiring fellow from middle-class Australia, who became prime minister and oversaw the beginnings of the dismantling of the White Australia policy and the referendum granting full citizenship rights to First Nations Peoples, before disappearing and presumably drowning after a swim off the Victorian coast, was the Harold Holt now synonymous with a lack of sporting success?

The legendary rugby league coach Jack Gibson was the first to use him. 'Waiting for Cronulla to win a premiership is like leaving the porch light on for Harold Holt.' Deadpan Australian humour.

The phrase can be applied to any situation when you're waiting for something to happen that seemingly never will. Leaving the light on for Harold Holt. A pointless exercise.

My favourite Harold Holt expression is a mixture of fact and rhyming slang. I was once dragged back from the airport to present an award to a group of museum volunteers because the government minister who was supposed to present the award, after dropping in to have his photo taken, had darted off. 'William,' the museum director told me on the phone, 'you'll have to do it because the bloody minister's done a Harold Holt, we can't find him anywhere.'

'Done a Harold Holt'. Done a bolt. Surreptitiously vanished.

•

My friend Bulldog, or the Dog as he is known to his pals, is your classic sporting man. Loves his footy and cricket, and the gees – horses, of the racing variety.

But just when you think you have a fellow like the Dog pegged, he has a few surprises. We're at the footy for a Doggies and Swannies clash, rabbiting on, until he puts up his hand and says, 'Wait there,' as if we're playing together for the Yarraville Fourths, as we did back in the day, and he's telling me not to run.

The Dog speaks mostly in cricket-ese. A dialect drawn from the world of cricket. When, for example, answering a phone call, he doesn't simply say, 'Hello, William.' The Dog speaks in cricket scorebook talk. 'Hello W D M G McInnes.' Using the initials for your first names and then your surname as it would appear in a cricket scorebook.

When it's time to say goodbye and end the call, the Dog says, 'Good luck out there,' as if you are leaving the conversation to go out to bat.

Even on this day at the footy, the Dog's love of numbers and cricket-ese is the basis of our chat about the prospects of the weather for the game.

'Give two to one there'll be a sprinkle from above, it's definitely a "Bunsen".'

To those fluent in such chat, this phrase means it's odds on for it to rain later. The sky above is like a cricket wicket described as a Bunsen, as in a Bunsen burner, rhyming slang for 'a turner'. Like a turning wicket the sky above will change character. It will rain.

After using his hand to tell me to wait, the Dog heaves himself up and goes over to an elderly lady whom he then helps into a seat.

When he returns, I ask who she was.

'Oh, you know, just an old chook from church, she doesn't get out much, but I make sure she gets a seat at the footy occasionally.'

'You go to church?' I ask.

'I do. Play it close to my chest, I swear like a trooper and will bet on two flies crawling up a wall but I'm also a bit of a holy roller. Not a God-botherer, but definitely a roller. Grew up with it all, so it's not a surprise. Got a couple of dog collars and some hot cross buns in the family.'

I nod. I like the Dog. A good man.

I like the way he said he's not a God-botherer, meaning an excessively pious or pompous person. A holy roller just rolls with their faith, it's their own business. A dog collar is a priest, and the hot cross buns are nuns. Good old Dog.

But it's when we talk about a left-footed player back in for the Swannies who is playing his 87th game, that I start thinking numbers.

'The mollydooker from Sydney is playing the Devil's number,' mutters the Dog. Mollydookers are left-handers, I can live with them, it's the numbers that make me scratchy.

Numbers are the hard stones of scientific theory and understanding. Sums either add up or they don't, a rueful fact understood thoroughly by the recent succession of Australian prime ministers. But when people become involved with numbers, these hard stones of science can be distorted and defy all logic and reason.

Lucky and unlucky numbers.

Seven has always been thought to be a lucky number across many faiths and cultures; in Christian terms God created the world in six days and rested on the seventh, so a day off is a fair enough reason to expect good fortune.

Apparently, there are seven heavens in both Judaism and the Koran, and in Confucianism seven represents the Yin and Yang combined with the five elements.

Sometimes different cultures have different views of numbers. I was leery of eight because of its ominous pool connotations, as in being 'behind the eight ball'. In China, though, eight is an omen of wealth and so is considered lucky.

Sometimes numbers have a more personal reason for existing in the fortune basket. When I was at uni, I had a part-time job as a spotter in a bingo hall where an old lady always got a bit excited if she saw 37 on her bingo sheet. One day I asked her why, and she said, 'Oh, love, I won the Christmas jackpot once, and thirty-seven was the last number called. I'll never get tired of seeing that beautiful thirty-seven!'

An old coot who was an ex-maths teacher and scorer at a cricket club I played for hated any binary number, calling them, 'A cack-hander's curse.'

I was very fond of 63 because it was the answer to the multiplication table nine times seven asked by a primary school teacher of mine who couldn't quite believe I came up with the answer.

Neither could I. Blind luck.

But when it comes to true idiocy, nothing comes close to 87 being the 'Devil's number' concerning all matters cricket in Australia. It's unlucky because it's 13 off a ton, the prized 100, the century of cricket, and 13 is top-shelf unlucky – its bad luck origins are multiple, but the most common is that 13 is the number who attended the Last Supper, where Christ was betrayed by Judas Iscariot.

I buy into 87 jitters completely and anytime I see or hear the number, I try and move on as quickly as possible.

At supermarket checkouts if the number appears in the cost, I'll quickly grab something else to add to the bill, thus escaping the dreaded number. But my grand mate PB is the true artist at embracing the 87 superstition.

PB has a list of cricketing disasters, all grounded in 87, including the startling admission that, because of these disasters, his worth as a cricketer was never acknowledged. This is a bit of a stretch because PB was a yeoman-like trundler as a bowler, and his nudging/nurdling batting technique was reminiscent of old stop-motion footage from a nature doco of some strange creature engaging in a courting ritual.

Over a few jars of his home brew, PB ran through a litany of his 87 misfortunes.

Wandering off after a golden duck, he had pondered how a batsman of his calibre could be dismissed so cheaply and when he checked his watch the time was 11.27 am. Of course, exactly 87 minutes after the start of play.

After another bewildering dismissal he worked out the temperature was 30 degrees or 87 degrees in the old money. Unluckily bowled middle stump to a veteran offie, who wore an eyepatch no less, PB noted the score was 3 for 29, and that 3 times 29 is 87. Not convinced?

Neither was I.

I challenged PB to come up with a connection between Australian cricket's recent ball-tampering saga and 87.

He smiled. 'Steve Smith was banned for twelve months on March 28th.'

'So?' I asked.

'The eighty-seventh day of the year.'

It might have been the home brew but he almost had me believing.

•

Sporting slang can even seep into matters of the heart. Both rhyming and otherwise.

It wasn't unknown for another pal to speak about her romantic success, or lack of, in racing parlance. 'Started strongly early on, got a good run, settled on a nice even money bet but pulled up short when I realised he'd die in the straight, definitely wasn't the sort to be a long-term campaigner.'

The funny thing was she had never placed a bet in her life but grew up in a racing household with her fair share of colourful racing identities.

I remember her telling me that at her high school formal she 'had to wear blinkers to put in a fair showing on a very heavy track'. Meaning that the fellow she went with wasn't much chop so she had to just concentrate on what was ahead of her, the way a horse who wears blinkers to focus its vision directly ahead would do, rather than be distracted by what was beside them. In her case her formal date. A heavy track meant a long night.

Maybe she should have considered breaking up. Getting dropped. Separating. Being dumped. 'Set free from the emotional guide ropes of a relationship.' I found that one on the internet.

It's something almost everybody will go through at one time or another: having your heart broken a bit or maybe a lot. There's no set advice about the whole shebang, which is odd really because some people go to extreme lengths to break up.

Henry the Eighth started a whole new church to get rid of one of his wives, which probably takes the energy and entitlement that a feudal, psychotic monarch who dabbled in divine right possesses, so I wouldn't suggest trying that.

I find denseness and having the sensitivity of a house brick can be an aid. Take my own good self. At a party I bumped into an old chum, and we banged on merrily until she reminisced about the time she broke up with me.

I stared blankly and uttered a line for lovelorn boofheads everywhere. 'You dumped me? Wait a minute, were we ever together?'

Thankfully, she laughed. After a moment.

It was better than me admitting what had occurred.

During press conferences the famous AFL coach Allan 'Yabby' Jeans was notorious for not wanting to answer journalists' questions, especially if he didn't want to give an honest answer or, more importantly, go anywhere near to addressing the subject raised by the question.

Jeans would simply pause, look solemn and serious – which was easy because he was a senior police officer as well as being a footy coach – take a deep breath and say slowly, 'I'm just happy with the four points.'

The four points being the amount gained on the football table after a win. That response also shut down the conversation. It became quite a famous catchphrase of his and was used by many others when not wanting to answer a question or confront an issue.

Cue to a young woman having a coffee with the young man with whom she had spent an active and hopefully mutually enjoyable night. The young man who she had been 'seeing' for a few months. The young man being a younger incarnation of me. And the young woman being a younger incarnation of my chum at the party.

Over that coffee, she asked a reasonable sort of question that reasonable people might ask when trying to ascertain whether there was any future in what was happening. Basically, she wanted to know where things stood.

'So, you,' she said warmly.

'Yes?' I said back, hopefully as warmly.

'Where are we at?' She smiled.

I tried to smile back.

She smiled.

'How do you mean?' I heard myself say, and even though I tried to say it warmly, it sounded a little like I was asking somebody if a suspension bridge over a yawning chasm was safe enough to cross.

She smiled, not quite as warmly as before but very nicely, and said, 'Well, this, us. Last night was lovely. It is always lovely. But, you know. Are you someone . . .' She paused and then went on, 'Are we something . . . that's going to be – something?'

I looked back at her and, may God forgive me, heard myself say slowly in a considered tone. 'I'm just happy with the four points.'

So, yes, I remembered when she dropped me, and it was lucky I ducked. I didn't fancy wearing the coffee or the coffee cup.

At the party, my chum introduced me to her husband. He broke into a huge smile. 'You!' was all he said. And he took my hand. 'Mate, I have wanted to shake the hand of the man who pioneered the Yabba Jeans approach to dying romance.'

They laughed and I had the good grace to blush and shake my head.

•

If you're planning a breakup, it's important to pick a suitable place.

Don't break up on public transport. I saw that play out on a train once in peak hour. It was sort of fascinating but agonising, especially as the train stopped in a tunnel for an eternity and had also been boarded by two energetic and pedantic ticket inspectors.

Just before a couple were asked for their fare details by the inspectors, the breakup got down to tin tacks.

'Why don't you want to be with me?' said one half of the soon to be former couple.

'It's just that I don't see myself kicking any sausage rolls in life with you,' said the other half.

The ticket inspector groaned as he heard that. 'Oh, mate, really? I should fine you for a line like that. You might want to go a bit harder with your meat pie.'

More footy rhyming slang: sausage roll – goal. Life goals. Life sausage rolls.

The inspector must have been a league fan for his 'meat pie' was rhyming slang for 'try', a score in rugby league. 'Going harder with your meat pie' in this case meant the young fellow should try harder with his choice of 'relationship termination words'. (That was off the internet too.)

Amazingly, I also once witnessed a memorable breakup at a karaoke bar. A young woman got up to the mic and quite pointedly sang Linda Ronstadt's 'You're No Good' to what everyone assumed was her dumped companion, then left with a flourish.

After she left, the bloke hopped up with a well-liquored and bellowing rendition of 'Kung Fu Fighting'. At the end of the song, before a silent crowd, he said into the microphone, as if he was interviewing himself post-game, the way kids do when they play before an imagined packed MCG in their backyard – or in this bloke's case, a payday Thursday night breakup at the karaoke bar – 'Well, congratulations, Declan, well played you, best on ground.' And he repeated in a mumble, 'BOG, BOG.'

•

On my Saturday morning walk, I patted the dog and thought of Chryslers and Vills.

An old teacher who used to oversee our interhouse sports carnivals with the jaundiced eye of somebody who'd seen almost everything there was to see, used to hand out appraisals of the performances he had witnessed on the volleyball court.

How he ended up being stuck with volleyball was anybody's guess. He certainly didn't teach very much technique. That was reserved for the good players who were all away with the actual sports teachers. And who, we all said, wanted to be good at volleyball?

This man was usually a chemistry teacher, but he would carry out his volleyball duty, standing in shirt and tie with a scorebook, running a little dry commentary and passing judgements on the performances he saw.

There were two types: Chryslers and Holdens. A pun on cars, which seemed to impress most students enough to pay attention to who might be who.

Chryslers were the makers of Valiants. And Valiants in the old chemistry teacher's opinion were the players who performed well. Holdens were the players who were 'Just Holden on'.

The idea of the Valiants caught on and, years later, my mate PB and I sat in glorious early spring sunshine having a coffee at Sammy's on the main drag at Redcliffe, banging on about rugby league. How dreadful the refs could be, getting misty-eyed for the days of proper scrums and generally mumbling old coot–style about league players, past and present.

Mostly past. For time was moving on and we had lost one of the Valiants.

Peter Leis. Champion inside centre for the Dolphins from the golden days of the Brisbane Rugby League comp. One of the most decent men to play the game.

He was a favourite of my mother's. 'As handsome as a movie star and strong as a bull, what more do you want?' she'd say.

I was surprised when I saw Peter Leis and his wife, Nerida, standing at the end of Mum's funeral service. I nearly asked him for an autograph, but resisted and thanked him for coming.

He nodded slightly and said simply, 'Knew your mum loved her footy.'

What a bloke.

Only a year before Leis had died, PB and I had attended a reunion game at Dolphin Oval where a host of old Dolphins gathered, and Peter Leis was among them. He wasn't very well but he was still 'Leisy', as handsome as a movie star and as strong as a bull.

PB went over to him and did something I'll never forget. He told Peter Leis how much he had mattered to him, as a ten-year-old. 'You were my favourite player, I wanted to be you. Even when we got thrashed, I wanted to be you. Thank you . . .' PB had trailed off.

Peter Leis had looked at PB and my old mate had continued. 'And you're still a hero. Thank you.'

Sitting in the spring sunshine with our coffee, I muttered to PB, 'Good you said those things to Peter Leis.'

We were quiet for a moment and then PB said, 'Here's to one of the Valiants,' and he raised his coffee.

I joined him. 'To Leisy.'

And then PB said, 'Mustn't forget the Vill.'

The Vill was PB's entry for the word of the year, mainly because he insists he came up with it. A Vill is a sportsperson or contestant ingeniously playing at the margins of the game with some success, but without physical harm to opponents, so not a villain but someone you grudgingly admire.

He gave me examples. 'Just like Wally Lewis in the '84 quagmire State of Origin.'

'Oh yeah. I remember.'

In rain so heavy and a pitch so waterlogged that Noah would have been plugging the Ark for leaks, the Queensland team were pinned on their goal line. Dropout after dropout barely reached the required ten metres. Enter the King. And also . . .

Enter the Vill. Wally Lewis barked to his Queensland players, making sure that referee Barry Gomersall heard, 'Stay behind the line, don't go over until the ball is kicked.' With Gomersall's attention fervently attuned to the goal line for infringements, Lewis *punted* the ball a solid forty metres! Pure Vill! Outside the rules, but certainly deserving of respect.

PB continued: Maradona's 'Hand of God' goal. All 165 centimetres of him managed to outjump 180 centimetres of Peter Shilton, palm the ball into the net, call for his players to celebrate uproariously with him . . . and get away with it. Crafty, cunning and sneaky, but you still have to admire it a bit.

'And the Vill we just lost.'

'Who?' I asked.

'Hugh O'Doherty.'

'Hughie O'Doherty!' I wanted to replace my espresso with an International Roast at the mention of his name, so far back did it take me.

Hugh O'Doherty, Valley's hooker of the '70s. I understood immediately. Hughie had the unnatural ability to steal the ball in a tackle. Players would take the ball up, be tackled by Hughie, then check to see if they still had their shorts, socks and boots for they sure wouldn't have the ball. He was a Vill . . . how he did it, no one knew. Sneaky, but he earned a loving respect.

Vill. It's a good word. I thought for a bit and asked PB, 'Have you ever been villed? On or off the field.'

PB pondered. 'It's the mid eighties, at the twenty-first of a girl I'm particularly enamoured with. Very keen on getting to know her better, so spent big on a gift, as big as a struggling uni student with a Vinnie's wardrobe could.'

PB charmed her for much of the evening, until he excused himself momentarily. On returning, she was engaged in an enthusiastic embrace with another 'friend' of ours. Big Trev.

'I love it!' she was saying. 'So kind of you.'

PB hung around for a while, waiting for an intermission. Didn't happen. That night was the beginning of Big Trev and the girl's relationship, leading to marriage. Only much later did Big Trev reveal that he hadn't bought a present, only a card – and he'd attached it to PB's gift!

Pure unadulterated Vill!

I laughed.

Thirty-plus years later Big Trev and the woman are still married with a horde of children, their first son named . . . Hugh!

Well played, Big Trev.

We raised our coffees again in toast to Valiants and Vills.

•

And I'd like to raise a toast to coaches who, while plying their trade, be they amateur or professional, add some spice to life when letting rip with a coach's spray.

'To cop a spray' means to receive a passionate assessment of your worth as a human being, or, more simply, to be angrily yelled at, usually by someone in a position of authority.

Like a coach.

Al Pacino's dressing-room address from the film *On Any Sunday* is part of boofhead heaven, but has been over-studied. The late Danny Frawley's legendary spray, available on YouTube, at a suburban footy team is more on track.

The traditional half-time spray is of Shakespearean quality: as rage-fuelled as King Lear, as inspirational as Henry V, as manipulative as Richard III – it all depends on the coach.

One coach of mine was a large red-faced man with a vast beard, foul temper, a daytime occupation as an irascible maths teacher with the nickname the 'Mad Swede'. This was aptly demonstrated by his tendency to scream his favourite coach phrase at any given time. 'What doesn't kill you makes you stronger! Stronger! STRONGER!'

When he was on song you could ask him, 'What's the time, Swede?'

And he'd scream, 'What doesn't kill you makes you STRONGER!'

Even his wife joked that that's what he said as they took their marriage vows.

During one meandering arvo of footy on our way to a predictable loss, the Mad Swede forsook his usual words and roared at the assembled team, 'Bugger the lot of you!' And stomped off.

Amazingly, we nearly won. Brevity on this occasion had worked.

When we walked in to the sheds after the game, the Swede sat quietly on the benches and said in a small voice, 'Thanks. Thanks for. Having a go.' And he nodded.

What a moment.

Part of the attraction of the spray is that there is usually a hint of desperation and frustration to the exercise because most coaches that I have had anything to do with have all been that species of human being who are ripe for either an explosion of frustration or an operatic aria of alarmingly heartbroken self-pity – middle-aged men.

I've always equated coaches letting rip with those truly tortured souls: the mathematics teachers at high school who tried to impart knowledge of the beautiful subject to me. Heartbreak mixed with fury mixed with the knowledge that time is finite and this is how they spend their time, trying to impart knowledge and to guide us – they might as well leave the porch light on for Harold Holt.

Once in mid-rant a lower-grades coach, who was a veterinary surgeon, demanded to know not only whose dog he'd run over, but also whose bed he had shat in, whose life he had inadvertently destroyed to be saddled with such a team of unrelenting shit. He got so worked up his mouth moved but no sound came from him. It was as if he were trying to do a Clutch Cargo impersonation. Clutch Cargo was a strange, almost nightmarish cartoon that incorporated a real person's lips on the drawn characters' faces. The lips were ruby red, either too big or too small for the character and spoke in exaggerated movements. I remember a winger telling me over a few drinks that he felt like pulling a few cones when the coach got into this state, 'Because that's the best way to watch that trippy cartoon with the lips.'

Eventually Clutch Cargo the coaching vet found his voice.

'If you were an animal I'd put you down, the lot of you. And you bloody forwards! I've seen a herd of cattle with foot-and-mouth who have more idea of how to go about packing a scrum than you.' Then he went eerily quiet, stood stock still and closed his eyes.

Somebody, I don't know who, let out a soft moo like a cow. People tried not to snigger.

Clutch stood with his eyes still closed. Then he mooed like a bull in rut.

All the team joined in mooing. The coach mooed back. God knows what people listening next door made of it all, but it was probably one of the most memorable sprays I'd been privileged to be a part of.

The other was one of those wistful sprays that sounded as if it were a scene taken from some bad Western when an old hand on the trail tries to tell a group of greenhorns about life. It almost needed a soft, sweet harmonica playing in the background.

It went like this. When the coach was a baby and he needed his nappy changed, his old man changed him. His dad was trying to be gentle; he was unsure and didn't want to be too rough with his infant son. He removed the nappy, cleaned his boy and looked down at his young child. He was, quite frankly, said the coach, moved by this vision of new life. The coach said his father stared in wonder at his infant son. And then the infant urinated.

'I emptied the tank. Pissed straight over my head and off over the table. Not a drop hit me. My dad said it was one of the most exceptional things he had ever seen. My dad, you've got to remember, was a cost clerk in the railways, he didn't get out much. But he saw enough to be impressed. And he'd say that story whenever he could, at birthdays, even at my wedding.

'I love rugby. I do, and I can tell you here and now that coaching you lot confirms something to me. I definitely fucking peaked as a man when I pissed over my head.'

And then he just walked out.

Generally, the spray is communal, so bearable. But when the coach targets you there's less fun to be had. The most suitable response to an individual spray is to say nothing and nod occasionally. After about twelve minutes of word-mangling, prolific swearing and finger-pointing, most coaches are cotton-mouthed and exhausted.

For some reason at school the best players always got targeted for a bake. One lad who everyone assumed would end up playing rep football at a serious level copped it the most. He just stood, showing no emotion. Eventually, after he left school, he stopped playing. Who could blame him? Men who were never as good a player as he was were always shouting at him. Shouting about what should have been done. Shouting about things they could never do.

Years later, I asked the player how he put up with all the sprays he had received.

'Easy,' he said. 'When they were going to get stuck in, I just started singing the chorus of that old Elton John song "Crocodile Rock" in my head. Pretty soon that's all I could hear.'

The chorus to that song had no words, just a falsetto 'La-la-la' repeated over and over again. I thought for a bit and laughed.

The player nodded. 'Yeah, kept me sane but after a while I just stopped listening to everything, the good and the bad. Fell out of love with the game.'

•

I remember another coach of mine, Sid.

After a truly half-arsed and self-indulgent effort in the field playing against a club that Sid had played for and coached, he addressed us in the change rooms.

Sid was a suburban toiler, the most kindly, gentle, avuncular person. He never took rugger that seriously, it was just a run around the paddock with mates. But he'd told us during the week he wouldn't mind us having a bit of a go against his old team because he wanted to show them a bit of respect. He wanted to be able to give them that.

At half-time this kind and gentle soul morphed into a creature full of apoplectic rage. He couldn't speak initially – his mouth almost made the veterinary surgeon's Clutch Cargo movements as no sound emerged. He sighed. Exasperated. Took a breath and then held out his hands as if he were displaying the length of a fish that got away. His hands shook and then he very slowly brought them together and grasped them tightly, shaking them as if his combined fists were a cocktail shaker.

Finally, as we wondered what was happening, Sid uttered very quietly and almost in a whisper, 'I don't know about you guys but I'M ANGRY! Can't you have a go?'

That was his limit, he could offer no more. We might have laughed another day, but not this time. It was Sid, a bloke who never asked for anything. We hadn't listened during the week, but we listened now. The brevity and gravitas of Sid's words worked.

The game meant something to him, and he needed our help, for us to do our job. When we went back out on the field, we had a go and won.

After the game, Sid didn't really say anything, just stood in the change rooms, nodded his head and gave us a thumbs-up. If there was ever such a thing as a gentle, almost meek raising of the thumb then we got it that arvo. It was almost as if he were embarrassed that he had asked us to have a go, to do what we were supposed to do. He was a truly humble and decent bloke.

Years later I bumped into him at a flower show. We chatted and laughed. When we shook hands at the end, he took a breath, went to say something, stopped and repeated the process. He Clutch-Cargoed again.

He still had my hand. Finally, he said, 'That second half, thank you. It actually meant quite a bit. I try to let you boys know if I bump into you round the traps.'

A random meeting a decade after, and nearly a thousand kilometres from where that Saturday afternoon footy game was played, and it still meant so much to him that he became a bit choked up.

I asked him how many of the team he'd bumped into 'round the traps'. He said about three quarters. He could have contacted one of us and then asked for his message to be passed on by family, friends, social networks. But that wasn't Sid's style. He nodded a goodbye and said he was off to see the orchids and I looked after him and thought, what a lovely human being.

•

Sport might not be everyone's cup of tea, as the Dog would say, but I turned back and had a bo-peep at the team that Daddy Coach had put out on the field and hoped that, wherever the contest might take them, they'd find a bit of support, inspiration and a lesson or two. And just to top it off, like the Dog at the end of a phone call, I murmured, 'Good luck out there.'

CHAPTER 6

THE BIG TIME

I can quite definitely say that I've had my limit of people – in public and in private – adding mayo.

It's a term I first heard on a cricket field when an opposition player who was kitted out as if he had just won Lotto entered the playing arena. Everything he had on was spanking, as in brand-spanking new. When he'd come out to bat, a bloke from the cover asked, 'What else did you get from Santa, Batman? You must have been a good Batboy.'

Dear old Bulldog, aka the Dog, saw the pristine apparition approaching the crease and muttered, 'All the gear, no idea.'

When Batman took guard, he didn't disappoint. Instead of just asking for his mark and then making the customary scuff on the pitch with the toe of his immaculate boot, he engaged in some strangely ornate and slightly exotic motions that looked like an interpretative dance movement.

He left the first ball alone, with a flourish one of the Three Musketeers would have been proud of.

There were groans from the slips cordon.

When he settled himself at the crease it looked like he was channelling a very bad martial arts 'master'. The sort you'd find on YouTube when you type in 'massive kung fu fails'.

His first stroke was a forward defensive prod that he held like a statue long after the fielder had picked up the ball and thrown it back to the bowler. The bowler took Batman's antics in and said, more in pity than anger, 'You pathetic flog. Why add mayo to a forward defensive?'

Later, when Batman was fielding, he took a regulation catch but added a couple of tumbles to make it look a bit more of a speccy.

'Adding mayo again,' sighed the Dog. 'A rissole is a rissole, you arsehole. It doesn't become a gourmet hamburger because you try to add a bit of mayo.'

Adding mayo is a simple enough concept to grasp. It's when you make something seem more than it is, even though it doesn't need to be more than it is. Make it seem a bit more of an effort. From the same genus as bunging it on, showboating, having tickets on yourself, putting on the dog and laying it on thick.

There's something irritating about adding mayo, especially when it comes to communicating. Politicians are major mayo-adders. Nobody could beat Donald Trump, the rissole who added spicy mayo by the bucket, like a toddler who can't control how much they pour from the bottle. Things were either, 'Very, very, very beautiful,' Or 'Very, very, very unbeautiful.'

But there was nothing like the home-grown efforts.

Everybody seems to think a press conference is their Churchillian moment, the time for them to release their inner wordsmith.

Scott Morrison was the sort of mayo-adder who believed more was less. Words would tumble out of his mouth like water from a broken water main, drowning any potential inspirational aims.

Invariably, there was a thumbs-up for the cameras and a mention of Jen, his wife, as if that was an answer to everything.

His government resembled a nightmare about Bunnings, where nobody could give you a definite answer for what you wanted but would also never shut up, sending you on to different aisles where everybody looked just like the shouty biggish guy who gave you an over-effusive wave and hearty, 'G'day!' when you walked through the doors. He'd hardly draw breath as he rattled away, reminding you where to go, listing things that were available, but they were all things you didn't want.

You'd ask for the garden section.

'See Scott in aisle forty-three, he'll sort you.' And he'd give you a thumbs-up.

You'd get to Aisle 43 and there he was again. 'G'day!'

'Weren't you at the door?'

He'd wobble his head a little and smile. 'Me? No way. I'm the Scott in charge of this section.'

You'd ask for the garden section.

He'd smile and tell you to go to Aisle 73, halfway down the left-hand side. And he'd send you on the way with a classic guarantee, 'That should definitely, probably, do the job. Most likely.'

You'd start to ask him another question, but he'd just turn his back and wander up the aisle.

And off you'd go to Aisle 73 where you'd find the biggish shouty man again. 'G'day!'

You'd ask slowly, 'Weren't you in aisle forty-three?'

'No, that was Scott! I'm the Scott in charge of gardening.'

In the end, you wouldn't get what you wanted but you'd buy something you didn't need and, as you'd walk out, the biggish shouty guy would wave at you like Forrest Gump.

'Scott?'

He'd smile and shake his head. 'No, not me, I'm Scott!'

You'd walk on and decide to get a snag sanger because that always makes you feel good. And then you'd see the community group running the stall: a biggish shouty man singing out, 'G'day! Do you want some mayo on your sanger?'

And then you'd wake up.

Luckily it was only a dream and there weren't Scotts in charge of everything. Or were they?

•

Depending on the day and the mood you are in, Bunnings can be an apex point of adding mayo. The day I went in search of garden 'utensils' was definitely a case of mood and day meeting as one.

What is it about garden tools? When I was a kid, there was the motor mower and the rake. That was it. Today there's an arsenal of weapons stuffed in my shed.

Next to cars and houses, these tools seem to have some influence in defining me as a man. They are indicators of the possibility of my manual competence. The possibly I might be able to keep the yards orderly and manageable. The possibility I can control what nature may throw at me. The possibility I might be able to use and control the tools.

This is adding mayo.

Some of the tools in my shed have hardly been used, like the electric chainsaw I managed to weaponise back to front. It turns out it is possible to put the chain on inside out.

Some tools, like the leaf blower, still rest, pristine and virginal, inside their box. Leaf blower? What is the rake for? Still, it's there if I need it.

But what is it about mowers? When did they become a thing?

After I attempted to fix my old Electrolux Weed Eater and it instead ended up as scrap, I set off to buy a new mower.

I was told at the mower section, 'This is the most important decision outside marriage a man can make. You've got to keep up with the Joneses.'

As a sales pitch it seemed slightly unreconstructed, but it is a perfect example of laying the mayo on thick. Mower envy. It exists, apparently.

Never being one to keep up with the Joneses, or even being concerned about who they were or where they lived, I simply said, 'I just want something that will start and cut. Maybe something electric?'

Apparently, the ones worth having cost an arm and a leg, and even then they weren't trustworthy.

I looked at things with names like 'The President', 'The Contractor', 'The Invincible', the 'Platinum Victor'. I said I didn't want a fleet of battleships, just something that would cut the grass.

'So you're one of those sorts of blokes,' the man said. What that meant I had no idea, but I took home a tidy little number that does the job. Mowers are handy things to cut the grass, not suburban status symbols.

•

It's easy to forget governments are made of people from the suburbs, cities and regions of Australia, people like me and you and those next door. So none of those people were expecting to have to deal with a pandemic, but it would have been better if the mayo hadn't had been added, and if it hadn't been laid on so thick.

When the vaccination program began, it wasn't announced with caution and a systematic approach. 'The eagle has landed,' former Health Minister Greg Hunt proclaimed, declaring 142,000 doses of the Pfizer vaccine had touched down in Australia.

Trying to liken a piece of governance to the 1969 moon landing, one of the truly great feats of human endeavour, by echoing the words of Neil Armstrong was never going to end well.

And when Greg Hunt doubled down, saying, 'AstraZeneca is cleared for lift-off,' he was just asking for it.

For such a capable politician it was odd he ended up resembling Batman at the crease. I could almost hear the Dog's sigh, 'All the gear, no idea,' when Hunt attempted to show the correct way to put on face jocks. It was almost as if it were a Mr Bean skit. The face mask went everywhere on his face other than where it was supposed to go. Although by the look on his dial, and the PM's, when they announced a few months into the rollout that AstraZeneca was to be bumped as the preferred vaccine, they looked like they might be happy to hide under a mask.

Nobody sets out to muck things up, but adding mayo is a sure way to tempt fate. Falling on one's arse, my father used to say, is a risk you take when you go about the business of being a human being. No need to make the impact bigger by skiting about what you are going to achieve. It's not easy being a public leader, especially during a pandemic, but I wish they'd go easy and try to keep their messaging as simple as possible. Sounding like a telemarketer selling steak knives when talking about public compliance or economic figures or vaccine rollouts defeats the purpose. Because, as everybody knows, no matter how well steak knife salesmen spruik, and however good the deal, conditions always apply.

Instead of adding mayo why don't people simply take a few on the chin, rein in the florid language and just say how things are?

The next time somebody steps before a microphone I hope they remember my old coaches — the Big Swede and Sid — and their brevity and sincerity, and then heed old Winston's advice, 'If it is a ten-minute speech it takes me all of two weeks to prepare it; if it is a half-hour speech it takes me a week; if I can talk as long as I want to it requires no preparation at all.' If a true conviction is to be conveyed, say it simply and succinctly.

•

Sometimes you come across a bit of showboating that you can't quite believe you've heard or witnessed, so rare and fine a piece of bullshitting that it grows larger and finer, like a rare old wine.

During the time I was at drama school at WAAPA in the mid to late 1980s, it seemed as if the success and optimism of that part of the world knew no limits. Perth, Western Australia. The home of a clutch of financiers and businesspeople who were legendary for skiting and carrying on like pork chops. For spending big and enjoying other people's money.

They showered themselves and sometimes the state with gifts that they never owned.

Alan Bond had a Van Gogh that was on the state art gallery's walls for a couple of months before it was basically repossessed. Grand buildings were left half-finished and even the America's Cup, won miraculously in 1983, went straight back to the Yanks after a failed defence in 1987.

Do you ever really enjoy stuff that isn't really yours? There was a slightly furtive feel to all the hedonism, as if it wasn't going to last very long. Maybe that's why when they came across the truly wonderful, people didn't really appreciate it. Perhaps they thought it might be less than what it was, like the bloke I encountered at the art gallery back then.

He looked like he was taking the piss. A turtleneck jumper, a plaid tweed jacket with leather patches on the elbows, corduroy trousers, loafers. To top it off he had a beard and longish hair swept back over his forehead like a fountain.

As he looked at the work on the wall he would point with an unlit pipe. When he wasn't doing that, the thing was clenched in his mouth and he would breathe through it, as if he were underwater and the pipe was a snorkel.

A wheezy whistle accompanied him around the gallery.

I was lying down on one of the broad couches that were dotted around the gallery. I was looking up at the ceiling, which was a maze of air conditioning hoses, when I heard a wheezing sound and I wondered for a moment if the hoses might be leaking. But no, it was the art fancier, his pipe heralding his arrival.

I was lying down because what was on the walls was fairly overpowering. Sidney Nolan. A seemingly endless collection of his work. The colours, the images, the feel and atmosphere filled the rooms and you. I wasn't quite sure what I was seeing, or how I felt about it, but it was, as my father would have put it, 'bloody something all right'.

Two women were looking at one of the Ned Kelly series and turned around when they heard the wheezing whistle.

We all watched as the art fancier with the pipe walked slowly around and took in the room like a detective taking in the scene of the crime. He turned to one wall, wheezed out a whistle and then, as he turned again, he sucked on his pipe for the time it took to almost rotate completely around.

He faced us. He stood still. Then out came a long wheezy whistle. He took the pipe from his mouth, held it in his hand and gestured towards all the assembled Nolans.

'Very derivative.'

Then he stuck the pipe in his gob and off he puffed, moving to the next part of the gallery.

After he left, one of the women said to other, 'That's the Secretary of the Kalamunda Art Society.'

As if that explained everything.

It was quite frankly bizarre. Everybody can think whatever they want of political figures, types of coffee and art on a gallery wall but to showboat so exquisitely was bloody something all right.

When somebody asks me what I think of something these days, I usually say, 'Very derivative,' and then I nearly always laugh, remembering the art fancier who was the Secretary of the Kalamunda Art Society. Whoever he was, he and his pompous pipe were a master in showboating.

•

It's an odd thing when you have a collision of art and sport. I freely enjoy both.

I loved playing sport – rugby, cricket, tennis, baseball, tiddlywinks and floatie catching. Floatie catching? Basically, it evolved from a uni party where anything that could float was thrown into a pool and had to be caught by somebody diving into the pool before said floatie hit the water. I don't have enough time to go on about it in detail, but I would like to take this opportunity to hail legendary floatie-catchers John Kendrick and Maurice Ware.

I played enough sport for long enough to make me walk like an old crock. I still can't help wanting to participate and even though I play golf like Basil Fawlty I still manage to have a good time. I had a hit of tennis with my son the other day and within an hour I was walking like the Tin Man from *The Wizard of Oz* in sore need of a grease and oil change.

Sometimes I walk down a street and up pops some old urge to tackle somebody in front of me, a case of Second

Rower. I resist but the memory lingers. Occasionally I can remember the feeling of a cricket shot or a golf swing, where timing and effort miraculously coincided to produce an all too infrequent connection of glory.

I can remember seeing Roger Gould dropkick a field goal against New South Wales at Ballymore. The sound his boot made, and the flight of the ball, was a thing of beauty. Like a Johnathan Thurston conversion from the sideline with its graceful arc curling through the posts, or Damian Martyn's off-drives and the sure, steady stroke of countless Olympic swimmers.

And I love watching sport live and on telly. From Merv Cook's length-of-the-field try against Wests Panthers at the Redcliffe Showgrounds to Tim Horan's World Cup try off a Hail Mary pass from Campo, to Cathy Freeman winning gold for Australia in Sydney, to Makybe Diva's third Melbourne Cup to the shy kid that barely said a word in all the years I manned the shot-put pit at Little Athletics and his bowed head and tears of joy when he won the event one bleak Saturday morning and made that grey day glow with his joy – I think sport is worthwhile and grand.

So, I can blame myself I suppose, or I could sort of blame Russell Crowe. And Clarice Beckett. But I can't help being a Queenslander at Origin time.

Let me explain. It's always wonderful to find new heroes. Clarice Beckett is an Australian artist from the early twentieth century who wasn't given the due regard that was rightfully hers during her lifetime. No grand recognition like Sidney Nolan got, whose acclaim during his living years was burgeoning on celebrity status.

Clarice Beckett had an overbearing father and invalid mother, both of whom she cared for as she went about her business of painting.

Her painting?

It's a joy being in a gallery and being so moved by what you see that you feel slightly elevated, as though you've been gifted a sort of a wisdom about simply being alive.

Clarice Beckett's work was mostly of landscapes, not sweeping vistas but of streets, pavements and modest beaches around where she lived. There's a magnificence in the everyday she captured and celebrated. The fluctuations of light, the sense of loss and of time passing, but also, marvellously, a joy of living in that moment.

What a top-shelf Australian. She lived a life, I suspect, full of grace and the sort of courage that won't grab a headline but matters because it's simply so ordinary.

The titles of her works are mundane – *Saturday, Wet Evening, Walking Home, October Morning* – yet so much richness and life is crammed into a seemingly humble subject.

Humble subject, wonderful art. A little bit overpowering emotionally but it's always good to be reminded of why it's lovely to be a human being.

A couple paused in front of a painting and sniffed. 'The Russell Crowe collection? Who would have thought someone like him with his football clubs would collect Clarice Beckett?' They laughed quietly.

There were a number of Clarice Beckett's works in the exhibition that were a part of the movie star's private collection and which he had loaned to the Art Gallery of South Australia. Unlike the Van Gogh that Alan Bond had on hire purchase, these were all bought and paid for.

I couldn't help myself. 'So, if you like footy you can't appreciate what you find on the wall in an art gallery?'

The couple, who were probably quite nice, looked slightly surprised, then nodded their heads. 'Point taken,' said the woman.

Good old Gladiator. I had his back. And then I realised he was a Blues supporter. A Cockroach. In the middle of an exhibition of great beauty I muttered a little too loudly, 'Queenslander.'

To try to make amends, I thought to myself, I'd raise a glass to Clarice that Wednesday night, give a nod to Russell and hope the Maroons slaughter 'em!

•

I'm not sure if anybody has ever called Russell Crowe 'Old Gladiator' but it wouldn't surprise me. Giving people or places nicknames is a great Australian pastime and it's also a prime example of how Australians invent and utilise language. If there is one thing that Australians do well, it is nicknames.

It's not only putting a 'y', an 'ie' or an 'o' on the end of a name, as in Jonesy or Hawkie or Johnno, although they count as much as any other nickname. It's when a red-haired person is called Blue: why? One theory is that the name derived from the tendency of red-headed Irish immigrants to get into the sauce and then put on a stink, or a 'blue'. Australians have a propensity to use one-size-fits-all labels, so a red-headed person simply became Blue. There's also the nice ironic explanation that blue is about as far away as possible from red on the colour spectrum. So calling someone the opposite of what they are has a perverse humour to it that Australians enjoy.

Sometimes nicknames can derive from straightforward geographical descriptions. Croweaters come from South Australia, Sandgropers from Western Australia, Banana Benders from Queensland. And I remember how my father would call Canadians Secondhand Yanks, because of their proximity to the United States, the fact their accent sounded similar and – mostly – because it irritated the bejesus out of his younger brother, who had immigrated to Canada while my father had chosen Australia to be his home.

Nicknames can be based around behaviour. During a season of lower grade cricket, I had a teammate who played like a right-handed Matthew Hayden and tried to murder every ball or get out in the attempt.

In fact, he liked murdering so much he was called Agatha, after Agatha Christie and her copious amounts of literary murder.

A university lecturer who had as many mood changes as the Melbourne weather was given a couple of beauties – Mixed

Bag or the Big Dim Sum, all because you were never quite sure what you were going to get – just like a mixed bag of lollies or the uncertain contents of any self-respecting dim sum.

I've had a few beauties. Came back from the theatre not so long ago after pretending to be somebody else for most of the day and just felt absolutely stuffed. Now, usually earning part of your living being somebody else isn't that taxing, but this was just one of those jobs where I was basically pushing the proverbial uphill.

My good friend gave me a great deal of comfort when I decided to whinge to her about my work.

'Oh, you poor petal, playing 'tendies makes diddums tired? Get a grip, you great ponce, people have to put up with a lot worse.'

So, no comfort for Ponce William – or Ponce Charming, as my friend took great delight in calling me.

Another addition to the cavalcade of nicknames given to me.

I always find it interesting to trace how a nickname might originate.

My good friend's young relative is in her first year of proper school and is a charming little kid who's going though one of those stages so many of us do, where you are a sponge and learning so much, so many new things, that sometimes it's hard to keep up and a few gaps and dropouts appear.

Like mispronouncing words. All of us have stories. My sister as a kid insisted on saying Father Christmas was Father

Tristram's. I think Christmas and Tristram's – the old iconic Brisbane soft drink company – sounded so similar she couldn't tell the difference. Or perhaps Christmas and Tristram's were simply both so lovely they could stand in for each other. In any case, in our house Father Tristram's became a name that was interchangeable with Santa, Kris Kringle and Father Christmas.

My youngest used to call a hospital a 'hospitable' and a hippopotamus a 'hippomotopamouse'. And my son at one time insisted on calling a *Star Wars* movie 'Esipode One'.

Of course, they all grew out of it and I'm sure my good friend's relative will, too. Although last Christmas she earned a nickname she won't shake for years.

We were playing a board game called Dog Bingo, where a breed of dog is called out and if you have the same breed in your allotted cards, you mark it off.

It was fun and doubly more so when the charming kid called out the dog breed Weimaraner, only it came out as 'Wee Murderer'. She joined in when we all laughed but I don't think she knew quite why it was so funny and that's the way it should be.

We all grow out of things but sometimes it's hard to leave behind a nickname that just emerges from out of the blue and gives so much fun to your family and friends. I've had some beauties in my life, which is good because I love being given and bestowing nicknames. Just a couple from my father, who had a number of names for me: Arse-part (I wasn't good enough to be the whole arse, just the bit down the middle) and Cabbagehead (self-explanatory); and from my mum: the Lucky Dip – because she just didn't know what she was going to get when I was pulled out.

Knockabout and fun, also oddly affectionate and full of love.

And I was given one from an exasperated rugby coach, who proclaimed I was like the Hardtop Cortina (a car that was also called the Poor Man's Torana).

Even so, I thought being called Hardtop was vaguely impressive and asked the coach what he meant.

'Well, Will, you look all right but you run like a pile of crap. Just like a Hardtop Cortina.'

A great moniker. And one that I am still adorned with to this day in certain circles. I've had others along the way: Foghorn Leghorn or the Big Chooky from my kids; from friends and work colleagues I was christened Tall Timber; from a pub owner who gave me a part-time job I was Pelican Shit (because I was all over the place); another footy coach referred to me as Bypass because I didn't play with much heart (in his opinion) and yet another called me Grandstand because he thought that's where I played my best football. And a personal favourite: Big Chief Fuckwit, which just indicates that sometimes I can carry on like a two-bob watch, throwing generalisations and half-arsed opinions around like hand grenades. And now there's Ponce Charming.

Sometimes, the journey of a nickname's creation is bewilderingly convoluted. Take a kid who I went to school with. For some odd reason, his name was Andrew Andrew. Before long he was Andrew Squared and then because of his double name he became New York New York, so good they named him twice, and then The Big Apple and Fruit, and then Fruit Fly and finally the rather epic 'The Fly!' – with the exclamation mark always thrown in when the name was uttered.

Now, that's a nickname. He told me at a school reunion that when he told his kids that at school his nickname was The Fly!, complete with the exclamation mark, his kids said it sounded like a character from a Marvel superhero film.

He shook his head while telling me this. 'I think they suddenly thought I was a bit more interesting, and they call me that now. The Fly!'

And he laughed. 'Kind of cute.'

For a truly singular piece of nicknaming, take the Pharaoh.

This was one of the nicknames created by my father, a linguist of invention. Dad had a regular customer to his hire business, a lovely old Dutch gentleman called Case Ankers. Case didn't like dogs that much – or, to be more accurate, he didn't like our sort of dogs. He and his wife had a couple of friendly though totally useless pugs, while at the McInneses' there was always a collection of enthusiastic kelpies and cattle dogs around, a tad too boisterous for Case's liking. So he would sit in his car and toot on his horn to let my father know that he was at the gate and could we please control our mutts. He tooted a pithy little series of staccato blasts, ending in a long-drawn-out howl, a sequence that, in its entirety, sounded like something Arnold Schoenberg might have been pleased with at his most atonal.

One morning there came the familiar tooting.

'Oh, it's the bloody Pharaoh,' sighed my father.

I had no idea what he meant. Why was Mr Ankers the Pharaoh?

My father sighed.

'Don't they teach history at the bloody school? What are we paying for!'

I looked blank.

My father sighed again.

'He sits in his ute, and he toots his horn.'

I looked even blanker.

My father shook his head and, not for the first time in our conversations, he sounded like he was talking to an idiot. 'He is a tooting car man. Tooting-car-man. Tutankhamun. The Pharaoh.'

I looked blank – and then laughed. It still makes me laugh today.

Linguistic fun and inventiveness, from our families and shared right throughout our society.

•

Sometimes, though, nicknames can merge with showboating, and we end up with the single-name syndrome.

Perhaps it was because I was telling a mate about the art gallery exhibition I'd been to that led us to start banging on about people known only under one name. Nolan, Beckett, Tucker, Smart, Whiteley. You know these folk through their surname; no first names needed. The same with Bradman, Murdoch, Trump. But that is not the same as single-name names. My pal had definite views on the practice.

'Showboating. A one-name name is pure showboating on a level that only somebody who lives in a bubble and has their heads firmly entrenched up their arse is capable of.' He paused. 'Which means it's something we are all capable of at one time or another.'

And it's not like Wazza from the local petrol station. When informed Wazza will be giving my car a service I know Warren Sykes, aka Wazza, will be on the job. But if Adele was doing the service, or Drake, Madonna, Rihanna, Usher, Meatloaf, Bono, Prince or Liberace were under the hood, I wouldn't be able to give a surname. Well, I could give you Liberace's, because it's Liberace, he flipped the theory and went with his surname. A flamboyant jewel-encrusted pianist who was a major twentieth-century popular entertainer.

Born Wladziu Liberace, he used to appear often on television, at which my father would invariably say, 'Looks like he plays on the wing for Wests.'

People change or repurpose their names for all sorts of reasons. Entertainment is littered with personalities who've changed their birth name in favour of a screen name or pen name. George Orwell was really Eric Blair, while Mark Twain was Samuel Clemens. George Eliot was actually Mary Ann Evans; Charlotte, Emily and Anne Brontë all used male pen names. Actors are notorious for changing names: Marion Morrison became John Wayne, Maurice Micklewhite became Michael Caine, Ramón Estévez became Martin Sheen while singer Katy Hudson became, for some reason, Katy Perry.

Funnily enough when a person goes by just one name, usually a given name, sometimes an exotic-sounding first name is followed by a mundane-sounding surname.

Adele Adkins, Prince Rogers Nelson, Rihanna Fenty, Drake Graham and Madonna Ciccone. These could be the names of anybody but using that one name frees them from the anybody and helps turn them into somebody.

What's even better is when the origins of a name are found. Bono, the U2 lead warbler and humanitarian, was born Paul Hewson. Sounds like a real estate agent. He came by Bono after a pal of his called him *bono voce*, which is Latin for good voice.

'Now,' my pal said, 'what's your single name? William's not much chop.'

I said, 'I have a loud voice, what's that in Latin?'

It happens to be *magna voce*.

Magna? I had an image of an old, busted Magna Mitsubishi that an old bloke down the road wheezes about in. 'I don't want to be a four-door sedan,' I proclaimed in my *magna voce* manner.

'Too bad,' said my pal, who started calling me Four-Door. This was slightly annoying. Even more so when he called me the Thane of Four-Door. This after the Thane of Cawdor from Shakespeare's Scottish tragedy. You know, the one whose title can't be mentioned because it might bring bad luck. Come to think of it, the title character goes by only one name; for safety's sake, we'll call him Macca.

My pal thought a bit and then smiled, which was a worry because that meant some smart-arse thought had amused him.

'Thane,' he said with relish. 'That's a good single name for someone. Thane.'

I agreed, though not for me. I paused and asked what 'boofhead' is in Latin.

My friend searched on his phone and smiled.

'*Boof caput*. Beauty,' he said, 'from now on, you're Boof Caput.'

Maybe Four-Door's better.

•

While I was out and about flogging a book I had written, a pleasant journalist asked me where I could be found 'on social media'. I replied that I had no idea. She was aghast. No Facebook? No Instagram? No Twitter handles?

'No,' I said.

'How on earth do you manage?'

'Quite handily,' I admitted.

She shook her head. 'How do you connect?' she asked.

I just stared.

'With people?' she said.

I admitted I managed well enough when I had to.

I have nothing against any particular social media platform, for indeed, it's just another way of connecting, catching up and sharing information with people. I am still moved by the image posted on social media of Queensland ambulance staff stopping to let an ill patient they were transporting to hospital take in the view of a beach and the ocean. Simply beautiful.

But, like most human endeavours, social media tends to descend to the lowest common denominator. And it seems to me to be a mix of people staying in touch with each other while at the same time being chock full of showboating, self-obsessed, look-at-me folk, as well as serial abusers, scammers, sycophants, conspiracy theorists and people who want to show how much weight they have lost.

And good for them.

But why skite about it with a series of inane and epically self-obsessed posts and images? Just get out and enjoy what you've done for yourself without inflicting it on everybody else.

It's this self-obsession that irritates me the most. If somebody of note dies there is invariably a post about the late person's worth and then a photo of the poster. It's as if the person's life that is being celebrated isn't worthwhile unless it is in some way attached to the person making the post.

I am currently working with a pal who is constantly, in his words, 'tending to the socials' – taking selfies, whipping off tweets and posting images on Instagram.

'It's the way of the world, Will, how business is done.' For him social media is more of a commercial proposition than a personal communications tool. He promotes an image of himself as a public figure that his 'followers' buy into and enjoy.

Follower. That is what people who connect into your social media are called. It's very cultish – you're the social media messiah and you have your followers.

Seeking affirmation through your social media posts seems to be a rather pathetic way of going about your business, but as my connected acting chum told me, 'Not everyone wants to be an old-school analogue curmudgeon like you, Will.'

Maybe he has a point, but I think there's better things to do with yourself than be an 'influencer'.

They are the remora fish of existence, attaching themselves to the great white shark of life; they feed on the bits and pieces of claptrap and vanities that seem to bloom everywhere these days.

My chum rolled his eyes. 'Mate, if an influencer mentions one of your books, they'll probably double your sales. Somebody tweets about you, posts something on Facebook or Instagram, you're rubbing your hands in glee.'

I said, yes, that it was most probably true, but I still thought they were self-obsessed bullshit artists.

My chum laughed and said, 'Not only are you a curmudgeon, Willy, but you are a hypocritical curmudgeon.'

I nodded and admitted that, yes, that was most probably true.

My feelings were crystallised a little more while I was waiting to cross a busy road the other day and a bus stopped in front of me. On its side was an image of a face. This face was flogging a perfume. And like an apparition it filled my horizon. Big lips, slightly parted, yet the jaw was teeth-grindingly clenched like a vice, hair flung back by some wind machine, eyes narrowed like somebody about to nod off to sleep after being tranquillised. This was not just a model but an influencer.

There was no flaw and no discernible human-like feature on the face, no pockmarks, pores, hairs or anything that looked like skin.

The image had been airbrushed and manipulated to achieve a desired end, but what was that end? If it was to sell the perfume, I didn't feel like buying it, certainly not for myself or for anybody else I might know.

I glanced up and above the tranquillised influencer's left eye sat a passenger, a senior school student who was taking a photograph of herself with her mobile phone. She contorted her face into some whacky tongue-popping mask, then laughed at her image and sent it to somebody.

It made me think the perfume-maker should've used the selfie-taker to flog its product, which made me smile.

As the bus rolled slowly away, the face on the bus seemed to have slipped into an even deeper stupor and I wondered what the model had been told to think while she had posed for the photo.

I had just left a studio after having a series of photos taken of myself for professional reasons. I had been told to smile occasionally, stand in profile to one side and then the other, then to sit and lean in a little.

I hadn't thought of much, except that I should've remembered to wear an ironed shirt, but it probably didn't matter as I always managed to look like an unmade bed even in a pressed suit.

I decided not to dwell on it too much.

These days people's social media photos have a few odd characteristics. They are so obviously paused, usually with pursed lips, vacant, well-practised smiles and a tilted head. Why do people tilt their heads in these photos?

The rules of these photos are that they usually make the subject characterless. It's heartbreaking to see these kinds of photos attached to a story of that person's demise.

And most are taken by the subject. Selfies, a word which Australia gifted the world. And nothing is more horrible than people losing their lives in the pursuit of achieving what they consider to be a superior selfie. For example, if there is a view from a cliff, the idea is to not just take a photo of the view, but somehow put the person taking the photo in the view, making the photographer the real subject of the photo.

It even has a name: selfie-cide.

An awful thing.

It used to be a bit of a deal having a photo taken. In photography's infancy the technology was so rudimentary that subjects were told to sit as still as possible so the camera's lens would be able to capture a clear perspective.

People dressed in their best, posing stiff and rigid in an artificial studio with hints of the outside world. The faces would be solemn and unadorned, and some images were so powerful they seemed to capture a person's soul.

Think of old images of American President Abraham Lincoln, where he seems to have a depth and wisdom of the ages.

I wonder what he thought about when he was having the picture taken. Probably wanted to scratch his nose or crack a smile or whistle a tune.

Oddly, when you have a passport or identity photo taken, you're told to remain still and not to smile, especially as face recognition technology works better on an unadorned image.

The more things change, the more they stay the same.

As a kid, photos were a big deal with ice-cube flash bulbs on instamatic cameras being rolled out as if they were gadgets from the future.

Instructions and exhortations to smile properly, normally and, above all, to pull no faces were barked out by parents to we subjects, meaning the resulting images were like wretched proof-of-life photos: a collection of grimacing smiles, dull-eyed stares and operatic half blinks eliciting parents' sighs about why good money had to be spent on developing photographs proving their children were idiots.

There used to be an awful wait after the film was dropped off at the chemist for developing, and a week later you gathered to see evidence of failure in having a good photo once again.

Now people take photos almost as naturally as they breathe in and out. Ad nauseam selfies. Or selfies taken through myriad filters, where things can be deleted, images altered, lips made fuller, manipulated not to look like reality but the way the photographer wants it to look. Speed shots of a series of the same image, then with help of an app one image is taken and offered as the best to use, not through human judgement but through an algorithm.

But my acting chum's words about me not getting the point of social media makes me think he has a point. It is a way of people contacting each other, a method to reach out and not just make coin, but to let people know what you are about, and let people know that they matter to others.

People can be strange in how they go about things, but that is a part of being a human, and sometimes maybe adding a bit of mayo isn't a bad thing.

Despite our misgivings about 'fake news' and our demands for truth and transparency, sometimes our interactions with people are based upon misunderstandings and long-running misconceptions, yet we allow ourselves to perpetuate the situations, not wanting to compromise a relationship or confront the participants.

My old pal PB told me of a bloke he bumps into every few months or so. They exchange pleasantries and this bloke always refers to their days of playing soccer together. 'Remember that game against Grange Thistle? They had to beat us to win the premiership, and we beat 'em!'

A couple of minutes of small talk, and off they go, content. But, according to PB, they *never* played in the same team. 'He retired a couple of years before I even started playing.' But why deflate a friendship with reality? 'He believes, and so should I,' PB says.

I was talking with another friend the other day and he mentioned, 'I saw Barbara Christian the other day. She looks well and asked after you.'

I was somewhat puzzled.

'Barbara Christian? You mean Bernadette?'

'No, Barbara, Warren's mum.'

'Mate, her name is Bernadette, not Barbara.' And so it transpired that, for over twenty years, this woman had graciously allowed my pal to refer to her as 'Barbara', never once correcting him as they spoke of weather, spouses, offspring, business, their town and fellow friends.

I'm as guilty. On set recently I listened to my old chum from drama school regale cast and crew with tales of our misadventures in a play we were in together. Some of these stories are slightly legendary in certain circles, and they always raise a laugh. The only problem was that my chum wasn't in the play and some of the stories attributed to me happened to another actor.

My chum was happy retelling inconsequential nonsense, people were enjoying hearing it. What to do?

Another actor who was in the play looked at me and winked. We both knew the truth.

Yet my chum nattered on; to call him out would embarrass him.

People are strange, but also kind. Why let innocuous memory lapses, misunderstandings, incorrect names and non-existent events affect a friendship? Truth and transparency are important but sometimes when we tell stories, we add mayo. Not to boast or talk big, but to grease the wheels a little, and maybe that makes the stories better – and the stories help us connect.

CHAPTER 7
CHANGING TIMES

Sometimes all it takes is having lived long enough to know that what somebody is saying is a load of tripe. Well, mostly a load of tripe. It is startling that, just by having lived experience, no matter how dense one might be, you are armed with enough instinct and enough memory to tell you that the latest 'thing' isn't that modern and isn't that dangerous and has probably been seen going round the block once or twice before.

I have lost count of the number of 'concerning social trends' that threaten our way of life that I have lived through.

Hippies, Trendies, Yuppies, Hipsters, Greenies and Bogans – all flame briefly across the night sky and disappear. They are all torch-bearers for various time periods: Hippies from the '60s and '70s, the long-haired free-spirited alternative lifestylers to the consumerist straitlaced mainstreamers of the system. Trendies were anyone who became instant adherents to whatever fashion or fad was the most popular at the time. Yuppies bloomed in the 1980s and were supposedly young professionals with a lot of disposable income to spend on things that weren't really that necessary. Hipsters were the too-cool-for-school millennials who brought an almost lobotomised passion to their cause. Bogans? Well, bogans and all their derivations – from cashed-up bogans, to middle-class bogans and the bogan elite – were basically everybody else.

Greenies used to be slightly unwashed types who would do things the rest of us couldn't be bothered doing. Chaining themselves to bits of machinery to stop some lovely clump of trees being torn down or a beautiful river dammed or drained. Somehow they became affluent inner-city dwellers who would vote for the Greens, feeling like that was enough to be worthwhile and then take off to their country or beachside retreats driving electric vehicles that were as much a staus symbol as a tool of climate activism.

All were the vanguard of 'concerning' social trends.

Usually, all it takes for something to be a concerning social trend is for people with microphones in front of their flapping mouths to have something to flap.

And people on the other side of the argument, who champion a social change instead of a concerning social trend, can't wait for the change to come and believe that we live in a society that is moribund, unjust and deeply unfair.

Woke-ism is the latest name for the list.

'You woke?' is a phrase I heard only recently.

It doesn't pay to be too literal with the evolution of language. 'Woke' is no longer just the past tense of wake; now it defines someone who is aware about what is going on in the community and, in particular, with matters pertaining to racism and social justice.

A lot of what is created by social media is as meaningful as a fart in a bath, but if some folks are going to create a word that expresses awareness about injustice and racial matters, then well done them.

This distinction is something people have differing views about. One person's idea of a joke can be another person's idea of being belittled.

Just the way some people think political correctness is simply good manners and caring about your fellow citizen while others think it is prime evidence of the fun police and an inhibitor to free speech.

Me, I am a moderate. Well, actually I'm a conservative old fart but I try to claim moderate status. This is often pointed out by people who know me, especially by two particular friends. One is a fellow who makes Andrew Bolt look like the Greens Senator Sarah Hanson-Young, and another makes Sarah Hanson-Young look like Andrew Bolt.

Both are lovely people who have views on either ends of the social and political spectrum and, Australia being Australia, they manage to sit around at the occasional dinner party without any rancour and are boon companions.

But somehow on a public level this idea that we can have differing views goes out the window, and this is when the tripe begins to flow and everybody becomes 'judgey'.

'We can't have fun anymore.' Patently untrue. Even as a COFA card-carrying member, I find that people who want to proclaim themselves anti-woke are more likely to be of an era that they feel defines them, and which they are therefore protective of, rather than trying to understand a situation that exists before them.

Nails is an acquaintance of mine, of similar vintage, who insists on still keeping up a nickname that was bestowed upon him by a footy coach who thought him as hard as nails because Nails ran into a goalpost head-first without any sign of physical damage inflicted upon him. As for the goalpost, it had a decided tilt to the side after being struck by Nails' melon.

Nails claimed he was given the nickname by friends who were envious of his ability to 'pull the birds' but also for the fact he had nailed the said 'pulled birds'.

There was never any evidence this was the case but that never let a blowhard like Nails cease proclaiming his 'swordsmanship' status for all who cared to listen. Pretty soon the name was said ironically but Nails didn't care.

The fact that he is still called this is slightly sad. And the fact that Nicola, his wife of nearly forty years, calls him this name is also slightly disconcerting, although she has a disarming way of explaining the situation.

'Oh, Nails is just full of shit anyway. I was his first and only girlfriend. If there were any others, he didn't learn anything from them, that's for sure. And besides, Nails sounds better than Kelvin, which is what his mum still calls him.'

Nicola also said that 'Niccy and Nails' sounded like 'a bad club act that had one song on *Countdown* and were never heard of again'.

Nails is one of those who can't stand how the 'fun police have descended on us all'. Everybody is 'so bloody politically correct'. At a barbecue where I happened to bump into him, he was bemoaning the fact that footy clubs now had themed nights for fundraising that were too woke and filled with '*MasterChef* things'.

What did that mean? I asked.

'Some bloke who knows about wine comes and talks about some wine and you can buy the bottles while another bloke who can cook makes meals to have with the wine. Club gets a cut of the sales.'

What was wrong with that? Had he wanted a beer and prawn night?

'Well, there's a time for that when . . . you know, when it's . . . is . . . a . . . genuine beer and prawn thing.' He shrugged his shoulders. It was astounding to see someone still do something that they did as a teenager in the same manner; it made time sort of elastic.

A genuine beer and prawn thing. 'Beer and prawn' was sometimes code for 'beer and porn', where a club night fundraiser would consist of a collection of footballers and hangers-on who would sit and drink beer while watching VHS tapes of blue movies. The tapes were of such dubious quality they would hiccup, lose focus, go unaccountably fuzzy and make little sense. Much like the audience after the cartons of grog had been sunk.

Nails couldn't really say what was wrong with the MasterChef night because it was enjoyable, and money was raised.

'Just different to the old stuff.'

I shouldn't have said anything, but I couldn't help myself.

'How do you mean?'

'When we had dress-ups and socials. You know, people would do acts. Fun stuff like that.'

I pointed out that most of the acts involved men dressed as women, sometimes in the clothes of the wives and girlfriends.

Nails shrugged his shoulders.

'You wore a crocheted bikini, Nails, one of your sister's,' said his wife. Nails shrugged his shoulders.

Nicola went on. She spoke about the sports days at primary school when all the schools on the peninsula would compete against each other and the year the students from the Redcliffe Opportunity School were included in the sports but kids still chanted insults at them.

'That's because we were kids,' Nails said. 'We didn't know any better, didn't understand. You grow up.'

'Exactly,' said his wife. 'Things change for a reason.'

'Well,' he took a breath, 'it's just when people have a go about being woke, it's like they are having a go at us, at me, at our parents, the way we did things.' He shrugged his shoulders.

'Things change, Nails,' his wife said, 'it's called growing up. It's life.'

'I fucking hate getting old,' he said suddenly. 'And talking shit. If woke means nice meals and good wine and people being looked after, I'm in.'

His wife gave him a hug.

I almost felt like giving him a hug too.

•

Diversity and inclusion, it seems to me, is a sign of strength. It means we all, as my dad would have said, should get a fair crack of the whip and cut each other a bit of slack, however we may choose to define ourselves. Being woke, or whatever you like to call it, is basically about having a few manners. There'll always be people who disagree, who'll feel that something is changing, something is being taken away from them, but as Nicola said, 'That's life.'

Luckily Australia is in a constant state of flux, evolving with each generation, and even though it might seem to some of us that the journey of transition is too slow, and too fast for others, we always seem to get to a better version of ourselves.

Gradualism, though, isn't for everybody so it's important to take a win when you find one and learn a little.

Driving along a freeway recently I pass a family who are in the process of moving. Their possessions in a trailer. A bag or two flies off the trailer and onto the road.

In my rear-view mirror, I see a twin-cab ute speeding up. Another tradie driving like a loon. I indulge in a bit of freewheeling generalisation. I don't understand why our roads are flooded with so many imported utes. Great swollen, steroid-enhanced things which are basically trucks, with names like Colorado, Ranger and Triton and other silly labels some marketer came up with. It makes me pine for the simple, commonsense elegance of the old utes like Holden HKs or HRs or Ford XYs and XLs. These imported obese creatures defile the name and whole idea of the ute, a peculiarly Australian interpretation of vehicles with a flat tray behind the passenger cabin.

I put my hand up and admit I drive a Swollen Viking Volvo car, with big comfy seats and mod cons, but it's a midget compared to the other things on the road now.

And I don't understand why people get so mad when they drive their swollen cars on the roads. Is it some correlation between the size of vehicles growing at the same rate the anger control of the drivers diminishes?

On the freeway, we're forced to stop due to some roadworks. The ute pulls up not far behind me. A big-bearded, fluoro-clad capital-T Tradie swings out the door. Big ute. Big attitude. Cashed-up bogan.

He runs to the family with the trailer. He's got something in his hands. Plastic bags, and a big teddy bear.

He's picked it up for them. Picked it up for a little girl who cries out and hugs the bear. The Tradie nods and walks back to his ute.

What a ponce I can be. And how lovely people can be.

•

Waiting gives you time to think. About the things you've lived through, about how things have changed. I found myself waiting in line for fish and chips at my favourite fish and chip shop, thinking about the 'treat' that takeaway food is. I still regard it with the excitement of a child. Way back when Kentucky Fried Chicken opened its doors (circa 1971), you knew you had 'made it' if your parents took you there. It wasn't called junk food then; it was 'treat' food because, well, it was a treat, rarely delivered and thoroughly anticipated.

'Wow! We're having Kentucky Fried Chicken *and* we can watch *GTK*?' GTK. Another acronym! Get To Know: 'young people's talk', and a title given to a ten-minute music show that aired on the ABC from Monday to Thursday. *GTK* began life as one of the more bemusing half-hours of television. Long-haired scruffnuts who head-banged away were followed by *Bellbird*, a fifteen-minute soap opera about the goings-on in a country town and then five minutes of *To Market, To Market* – the stock and food prices at markets, hosted by a large bald man in a safari suit. He was jolly and happy and was dubbed 'the big happy bastard' by my dad. Or BHB in acronym chat.

GTK was always on but interrupted by the mumblings of my father about some of the acts featured on the ten-minute nod to youth culture: 'He's got more hair than he has talent,' and the iconic description of Liv Maessen, a singer from Tasmania who was very tall with a very deep voice performing 'Knock, Knock, Who's There?' As she warbled away, my father took her in and said rather cryptically, 'Must be the Senior Constable's Saturday night off.'

My mother yelled, 'Colin!'

My father said, 'Well, look at him,' and then both my parents laughed at Snr Constable L. Maessen.

A Kentucky night meant it was someone's birthday. I can't remember whose, but I do remember *GTK* was watched without any interruption from my parents. A special night indeed.

By the time I was twelve, *GTK* had disappeared into the ether and was replaced by *Countdown*, so I had a Kentucky birthday without *GTK*, but I still knew it was a treat.

Later down the track, at an impromptu dinner at uni celebrating somebody's twenty-first, it became known as the 'Dirty Bird'.

Years later, when my son was turning twelve, he asked if he could have the 'Colonel' as a birthday treat. It was a respectful nod to Colonel Sanders, who had begun the franchise in America all those years ago. I always thought that 'Colonel' had a matey, rather friendly feel about it, though

Popcorn Chicken was forbidden from the birthday menu as my son's mother quite reasonably considered no living thing should become popcorn anything.

Could the same be said of pies? The meat pie is more than just a takeaway item; it is a major meal in its dominant arena: the footy.

Although there's a clutch of assorted 'nibblies' available whatever your chosen code may be – from hamburgers, to chips, dim sum, doughnuts, Chiko Rolls, ice-creams, hot dogs, and sandwiches – it's pies that rule the footy roost. They are invariably ridiculously priced and can be served and eaten at varying temperatures. From the scalding hot pie that elicits sounds and facial reactions right from Curly's playbook from *The Three Stooges* to that awful feeling when you take a couple of bites and the 'pie' turns into a meat-lovers Paddle Pop.

If you get a bad pie when playing footy pie roulette, you and anybody near you will know about it, because it's the gift that keeps on giving.

Pies are many things to many people because, according to Food Standards Australia New Zealand, Australians eat an average of twelve meat pies a year, which rounds out to 270 million pastry parcels of chance.

I get sentimental about the pies of dear old Marle Juster, a lovely man who had a clutch of bakeries on the Redcliffe Peninsula of my youth. His creations were of such lustrous quality all pies since have been measured by them.

Footy pies don't occupy Marle's rarefied air but are instead a pie subspecies unto themselves and part of the footy experience. For instance, they can be foodstuff and also a handy metaphor in giving a bit of spectator advice. I remember last year hearing some goon from the crowd scream out to a certain fly half that his kicking game stunk 'almost as bad as my pie!'

And a friend of mine has a way of rating the quality of a rugby league game in terms of pies. A Five Pie Game is of the highest quality while a One Pie Game is the other end of the spectrum. The dreaded Dropped or Split Pie Game is one where the result is determined by the lamentable decisions of the match officials.

The pie is also the basis of one of the great foodstuff sledges on someone's appearance. If someone may not be the most attractive person, then it may be said that 'they have a face like a dropped pie'. Of course, the mango runs a close second: 'They've got a head like a sucked mango.'

It could only happen in Melbourne I suppose, but I was at the MCG watching an Origin Game – a Dropped Pie Game, unfortunately for the Maroons – when I noticed there were a variety of footy pies available. Your bog-standard meat pie then some more refined options: beef burgundy, curried duck, green curry, and, astonishingly, a vegan meat pie.

I couldn't help myself and decided to bravely carry out a taste test by indulging in a bog-standard meatie and a vegan meat pie. Both with sauce, of course. I was astounded further that both pies tasted as bad and as good as each other. Evolution of the highest order. Couldn't spot the difference.

As I was lost in this reverie, I received a text from PB.

'Mate, Anchorage bakery at Newport — best salad sangers on the peninsula; pricey, but quality has a price. Mate, they are the salad sanger equal of the Woody special burger.'

If there is anyone who knows the value of a dollar it is PB, and if there is anyone who appreciates a salad sandwich it is PB, so punters take note.

We all have our favourite haunts, often directed by memory, and on the corner of Sutton and Violet street in Redcliffe in the 1980s was Woody's takeaway. Best. Hamburgers. Ever. A beef patty, lettuce stained with beetroot juice, black-ringed onions, tomato, cheese and a sauce that was ambrosia. Woody's is long gone, but I am still waiting for its resurrection. The space has been a manicure shop, a photography store, an art studio, a pale imitation of an American diner, where quantity trumped quality, and a vacant store for a long time.

The bloke in front of me at the fish and chip shop snapped me out of my contemplations: 'Much calmer now, no rush, keep your distance. Same as in the pubs. Used to be a fight for the front of the bar and a fight *at* the bar. People, hey? I dunno.'

Now we wait, in line for my barra and chips with the deep-fried sweet potato and corn cob . . . life is often just waiting . . . waiting for a burger as good as the Woody's special. Waiting. The burger will never be as good, but we wait. Still waiting.

I remember the Italian place down the road from where I lived in Melbourne. It made the best spag bol. It is right to use the slang word for spaghetti bolognaise because the spag bol from this place had a meal feel all to itself. It was cheaper and bigger than the one served in restaurants.

I was put on to it by a man called Vince who used to have a fruit and veg around the corner. Vince still helps out in the shop, which is now run by his son and only sells organic produce, along with organic coffees, teas and other assorted organic stuff.

The little shopping strip where the fruit and veg is located used to have four bank branches along with a bakery, butcher, hardware shop and newsagency.

Now there are coffee shops and restaurants: Chinese, Vietnamese, Thai, Indian and Japanese. There are two barber shops – one a holdout traditional buzz cut and clippers joint, the other heavily hipster oriented – and no bank branches.

Things have changed.

The last time I was at the fruit and veg shop another customer was talking to Vince about a new restaurant opening up. A grill.

The customer said it looked good.

Vince sniffed. He said it was in the old National Bank branch. 'It'd better be good, bad vibes there in the old bank.'

The customer laughed and asked Vince if he didn't like the banks.

Vince shook his head. 'Bloodsuckers! What did the bank ever give you?'

The customer nodded and Vince looked at me. 'Give you nothing!'

I thought a bit.

Everyone is getting stuck into the banks now. No matter how much they spend on advertising telling you how they'll always be there for you, in bad times and good, providing rescue helicopters to winch you to safety, everybody has horror stories about banks.

How banks are perceived entered the nation's vernacular. If you weren't a very generous type, say a referee who wasn't showing any charity to a particular team, then you might be referred to as being as 'Generous as a well-fed banker'.

If a banker is well fed, he's eating all the profits and isn't likely to share.

'Me worst mate,' was a homeowner's lament about a bank. The worst mate was the bank who held the mortgage; everywhere you go your worst mate isn't far from your thoughts.

It wasn't always the way. A bank manager used to be up there with a doctor, a dentist, and a chemist as one of a suburb's more prominent citizens.

Now banks are big corporate machines. They don't belong to little suburban shopping villages; they're voices down telephone lines or a click on your phone or online services.

As a little boy, I used to go with my mother to the bank every Friday afternoon, when she'd get money out for the weekly shop over a happy chat with the teller.

It seemed like a nice place to me back then, but later my mother would say a bank is only a nice place when you've money to take out and put in. I found out what she meant later in life. I'd see people disappointed, angry and lost in banks. It's a terrible thing to see someone crack it in a bank or at an ATM.

What do banks ever give you?

And then I remembered. Moneyboxes. They'd hand the things to parents who would in turn hand them on to their kids. One mate said he even got one as a stocking-filler at Christmas, which he took to be a little bit on the cheap side, but a stocking-filler is a stocking-filler. Or perhaps you would be given one at the Ekka when you walked through the Industry Pavilion and passed a bank display. A mixture between a lesson in saving pennies and building brand loyalty – a marketing exercise to attract children to a product, a little like the toys in the breakfast cereals of my youth. The banks all had a 'kids' range of products to entice customers at an early age. Novelty moneyboxes were all the rage.

My lord, those moneyboxes. A tin replica of the Commonwealth Bank in George Street, Sydney, was matched with a plastic blue elephant which was described by my aunt as 'a knock-off Henry Moore sculpture'.

The National Bank had a blue safe complete with a combination lock system and there seemed to be a parade of rather unhappy-looking Australian animals with coin slots in their heads or backs and, not so long-ago, creatures called Dollarmites.

The Bank of New South Wales (Westpac these days) had a base-level model which was a treasure chest with a slot in the top, and a showpiece one in the shape of Donald Duck. The first account I had was a Donald Duck and Friends Passbook from the Bank of New South Wales and the fact I still have it, with evidence of only one transaction, a deposit of $2.57, shows a certain lack of interest in pecuniary matters.

So long ago, another Australia. Who even remembers Donald Duck these days?

I laughed. Vince looked at me.

'Come on, Vince,' I say. 'A bank gave me a moneybox once.'

He looked at me and then laughed.

He went out the back and came back holding, of all things, a National Bank plastic safe complete with little combination dials. He must have had it for years.

'Me too,' he said and then added, 'bloodsuckers!'

Banks. Odd beasties. I remember when they were only open till four o'clock in the afternoon and the idea of staying open till 5 pm on a Friday was breathtaking. Everything was done over the counter, person to person, with little ledger books detailing the money in your account.

Banks seemed unchangeable until the ATM, the hole in the wall bank. A pal once told me how her father, who was in charge of rolling out ATMs across Brisbane, would take family and friends on a drive to show them where these 'space age' machines would be placed.

Those were the days of Gregory's street directories, where whoever was navigating would risk paper cuts while frantically turning pages in search of the quickest route to the proposed sites of the space age entities.

Now even ATMs seem a bit prehistoric, for nobody really uses cash much anymore.

Swiping or tapping your card or phone is very modern, very space age and convenient – except when the bloody online banking goes on the blink.

I thought I'd give PB a bell and have a bit of a yack while I waited at the fish and chip shop.

We said our hellos. He asked me what I was up to. I told him I was waiting for my fish. Told him his mention of his salad sanger and Woody's had struck a chord.

He repeated the name Woody's as if it were a fine wine.

I asked him how he had gone in the recent bank outage.

'Fine,' he said.

'Lucky you,' I said.

'Cash,' came the monosyllabic reply.

I laughed. 'Who has cash these days?'

'You idiot! Heaps of people still use cash! We're called Luddites or antediluvians.'

PB went on to tell me how, when it's time to pay for something and someone thrusts a device (which PB calls 'the thingy') in his direction, expecting him to flourish a piece of plastic, 'This is the moment when one century collides with another. I slowly and most assuredly open my wallet to reveal the rainbow of colours that constitutes our currency and extract a redback. "Will cash do?" I innocently enquire. After the initial shock, the quest for the attendant is now to "give change".'

I laughed again.

'I don't know why you are laughing. Cabbage is currency. If you don't have folding, then you don't have money,' he said.

PB baulks at establishments only allowing cashless transactions. Such a lack of privacy. PB and his wife diligently take turns in checking through their bank statement. 'Still delivered by snail, naturally!' he almost crows.

His wife, with slight incredulity, recently asked him about a mysterious item that had caught her eye. 'What's this almost two hundred dollars for drinks at Toowong soccer ground?'

Naturally she thought something might be amiss, perhaps a phishing attempt (an attempt to acquire sensitive bank data).

PB uttered a feeble reply: 'Er, I shouted the team. We drew. Won't happen often.'

On the phone, PB tells me the story, 'My privacy invaded, all because I couldn't pay cash.'

And, according to PB, it's impersonal to add a tip when paying with your card. How about slipping a Henry Lawson into the waiter's hand as you thank him for the lovely service?

'More importantly,' I ask, 'will buskers survive?'

There is no response.

A bleak day beckons – has probably already arrived – when buskers have 'the thingy' alongside their CDs for sale. Do they stop their song, complete the transaction, and continue?

What if they're halfway through the extended coda of 'Hotel California'? They might have to start that dirge all over again.

PB's got a point, somewhere in there. I'll make sure there's folding matter in my wallet from now on.

'Lesson learned then, Big Fella.'

•

Just as I hung up, a punter walked out with his takeaway meal. He couldn't help himself; well, who could? He reached through the wrapping and went to sneak a sly chippie or two. They were hot, a sigh of steam came out of the little tear that had been made. Maybe too hot for a neat chip sneak. The punter winced a little and juggled the chip in his free hand before it fell to the ground.

It lay there. A golden, stubby little piece of joy lost. The punter looked down at the fallen chip.

'Shit a brick,' he said matter-of-factly.

He bent down, balancing the rest of the meal in the crook of his arm and he gently picked up the chip and dropped it in the bin.

'Bit of a waste,' he said to the assembled crowd before he got into his car and drove off.

Swearing. Australians are good at it, even if it's inadvertent.

The Deputy Premier of Queensland, Steven Miles, had a mispronunciation a while back, gifting us one of those moments people love to get het up about. The dropping of a C-bomb in relation to the then Prime Minister Scott Morrison. Mr Miles claimed he stuttered and mispronounced a word. As far as these things go, it's better to take people and their explanations at face value – it can happen to anybody. Like the former PM himself, on camera, mangling the pronunciation of then Federal Health Minister Greg Hunt's name and bequeathing a C-bomb for posterity.

It was not unknown for Greg Hunt's name to be a bit of a swearing stalking horse after the PM's slip of the tongue. At my local supermarket, which was in Greg Hunt's electorate, the young blokes who were stacking the shelves were engaging in a bit of banter and skylarking.

One, who knelt on one knee, was stacking packets of breakfast cereal on a bottom shelf and another stacker was picking that very cereal packet off the shelf and giving it back to the kneeling stacker. A time-honoured bit of supermarket nonsense.

When the kneeling stacker finally worked out what was going on, he burst out laughing and told his equally gleeful co-worker to 'Stop being such a Greg Hunt.'

He ran the names together, Scomo fashion, and elicited more laughter.

A bit of cheek and fun.

Even legendary NRL commentator Ray Warren got a case of mixmaster in mouth when he dropped an inadvertent C-bomb as he loudly proclaimed the first initial and the surname of Queensland origin fullback Karmichael Hunt. All on YouTube for posterity.

The C-bomb's about as nuclear as swearing gets, and it still astounds me when people use the word casually in general conversation or in public.

Waiting for a coffee, I was sitting in the sun with other patrons of a busy bakery that doubles as a more than useful coffee shop. Lots of demographics on show. Boofheads like me. Well-dressed boofheads. Young parents. Teenagers. A couple of nannas and grandads by the look of things, and women in their early twenties.

One young woman was on the phone with earbuds in, talking loudly. I don't know who Rohan is, but apparently he was behaving like a ripe C-bomb. Yeah, she said, he's always had that in him because his brother is such a C-bomb and his dad as well. All C-bombs.

On and on she went, as if the C-bomb was like 'You know?' at the end of a teenager's sentence. A habit.

Some of the older people were wincing at the words. Apparently even Rohan's mum was a C-bomb. She just pretended to be nice and care, but she was just a C-bomb with a nice smile.

Nobody said anything and the young woman seemed oblivious the entire time.

A mate of mine said she had no problems using the C-bomb in conversation because, after all, she is an owner–operator, but also felt that one shouldn't overuse it. Men can often substitute the C-bomb for 'mate' and drop it effortlessly into conversation, but usually only in the company of men. So it came as a bit of a shock recently when an old fellow in a late model Mercedes wound down the window and gave me both barrels for no discernible reason.

I had crossed at an intersection with lights when the pedestrian lights were still flashing red. But this, combined with the fact that the driver's light was still red, didn't seem to matter to the old coot with the Merc.

He dropped C-bombs on me.

I maintained a certain dignity and suggested, 'Go for your life, champ, you are all class.'

And he exploded with, 'Don't you champ me, you f-ing C-bomb.'

I replied, 'Okay, chief, no champ for you.'

He nearly went into meltdown.

'Procreate you! You female orifice, you male appendage attached to your head. Procreate you!'

I couldn't help myself and came back with the time-honoured foolproof boofhead retort that Oscar Wilde would have been proud to have authored.

'You are!'

If he went into meltdown before, now he was apoplectic.

Why? Who knows. People seem ready to go all-out with a verbal attack at the slightest provocation these days. Perhaps a pent-up collection of grievances builds and when an excuse to break the dam wall of politeness presents itself, they crack hardy. Or perhaps there is just no filter. No control. No awareness. People walk around in their own little bubbles.

Certainly, the Merc driver didn't seem to have anything to really complain about: he had a nice car, nice clothes and magnificent hair.

Cursing and swearing is pretty bargain-basement behaviour.

Better to leave the nuclear option as a threat and use a bit more vocabulary. Non-curse words can occasionally be rather fun.

'A real fart in a bath,' sums up the emptiness and nonsense of a person, especially a pollie. Just like a fart in a bath there's a bubble of noise and excitement but not much substance. If there is, somebody else has to clean it up.

Good old-fashioned terms like 'droob', 'drongo', 'hammerhead', 'arse-part', 'clown', 'galoot', 'fool', 'tripe-hound', 'goose', 'donkey', 'flog parrot' and 'boofhead' should get more of a rollout.

Or maybe go homemade and create your own, but don't go nuclear with the C-bomb.

CHAPTER 8

WASTING TIME

It was left to dear old Bob Hawke, or 'Hawkie', as one of the longest-serving Australian prime ministers was universally known, to exquisitely describe the doubts some held about the leadership abilities of future PM Tony Abbott.

'Tony?' Hawkie laughed to himself a little. And said with a slight sigh, 'Oh, Tony. Look, I don't mind Tony personally, he's not a bad bloke. But as I said during the campaign, he's as mad as a cut snake.'

Well, Tony Abbott has his defenders, and he is not without certain qualities, but when his relatively unsuccessful two-year stint as PM came to an abrupt end, many remembered Hawkie's words. Especially after Abbott inexplicably awarded Prince Philip, of all people, an Australian knighthood, which basically sealed Tony's political fate.

Tony Abbott was a Rhodes scholar, so intelligence wasn't the problem, but what he did was unaccountably tone-deaf and stupid. Bringing back knighthoods and damehoods was bad enough but to give one of the silly bloody things to the Queen of England's husband – Prince Philip – a bloke who had more imperial honours bestowed upon him than he had had hot dinners, was top-shelf fool behaviour.

And here's the thing: if you behave like you are as silly as a wheel, or as mad as a cut snake, or a sandwich short of a picnic, it doesn't mean you are always this way. As the late Shane Warne put it, 'Just because I do dumb things sometimes, it doesn't mean I'm stupid.'

Appearing stupid and as silly as a wheel is part of being human.

Walking through an airport, I was suddenly struck by how people conduct themselves in public now. It's probably been happening for a while, but I only realised when I saw it en masse.

What I noticed was people talking to themselves. Or, more accurately, appearing to talk to themselves. A whole terminal of people staring off into the distance and banging on, rambling away to invisible friends. It looked like everyone was off with the pixies.

It reminded me of how my parents used to say such behaviour was left to certain local residents of the town where I grew up who were lovely people but weren't quite right and behaved like every day was 'Pension Day', whatever that was supposed to mean. One definition was that Thursday was the day that 'the allsorts and short ends' got their pension cheques and would head out in an overly excited manner to the bank.

I remember one man, always dressed in white, who would catch the early bus to Sandgate on a Thursday, the same bus I took to go to school.

There he would stand, looking quite smart, as if he were either heading off to go lawn bowling or to do something in a laboratory, always mumbling a set of figures, which were the times from the bus timetable.

If the bus was late or, more unusually, early, he would board the bus and say quite loudly, and to nobody in particular, the time that bus was meant to arrive according to the timetable.

He had a deep voice and sounded not unlike Yobbo Ahab, the Danish architect.

There seemed to be so many lovely people muttering to themselves at bus stops, on benches outside the shops, or the odd 'soliloquiser', another creation of my father that described those amongst the populace who engaged in a bit of Shakespearian behaviour. The old bard was fond of his characters talking to themselves. A soliloquy is when a particular character stops addressing others in the play and rambles off on some inner monologue aloud.

The people in the airport terminal were all talking to someone at the other end of a digital connection on their mobile phones. But their almost invisible earbuds and headphones had turned them into soliloquisers.

Sometimes you can misguidedly think some of the conversations are addressed to you. I nearly jumped out of my skin when someone behind me said, 'I've really missed you, you know how I feel.'

I turned rather quickly and even though he was keeping a suitable 1.5-metre social distance, a rather large and hairy fellow, with a sleeve of tatts that the former Collingwood champion and epic tattoo enthusiast Dane Swan would be proud to wear, was talking to somebody in rather intimate tones. The problem was he was talking quite loudly.

Even worse is somebody howling down a phone as if they're yelling to somebody at the other end of a paddock. These soliloquisers are usually passing on the most banal and tedious details at high volume.

Back in the day before mobiles, phone booths gave callers some degree of privacy.

Now all that's gone out the window and people just bang on, so immersed in their conversations that volume and discretion, and even the presence of other people, aren't really considered. It is, I suppose, just a different way of going about life.

I looked around at all the soliloquisers and couldn't help but laugh. What a bunch of galahs.

Anybody could look like a galah when you talked to yourself. Look at Hamlet, he soliloquised like nobody's business and everyone thought he was mad. And even a self-referencing man of action, who soliloquised in rueful sardonic wisecracks while saving the planet looked a brick or two short of a load. Perhaps it was his mullet. MacGyver.

•

When you behave like you are as silly as wheels, it helps to have a role model. Mine is MacGyver. The legendary mullet-maned American small-screen secret agent of the 1980s who would successfully get out of tight spots by using all manner of everyday items.

'To MacGyver' is to be inspired by having no idea but deciding to take a punt. Even utilising man's best friend.

That's a bit gender-specific perhaps, although it strikes me that men, in particular men like me, treat man's best friend very shabbily at times.

I'm not talking about dogs. I'm referring to man's other best friend: the microwave oven.

Some say they don't heat evenly, don't kill all the bacteria from old meals, but I'll take a punt on the radioactive roulette wheel of stodge.

Microwaves used to be a thing of the future. A mum of a high school friend said, 'The really good ones are only ever on *Sale of the Century* as a prize, no way we could ever afford a good one.'

Sale of the Century was a game show that tempted the viewers with unimaginable prizes, like a 'good microwave'. A time capsule of another Australia.

I first became aware of the concept of microwaves from television shows like the animated series *The Jetsons*, set in the future, where, with a touch of a button, something would be created in no time at all.

My first real use of the microwave was at petrol stations on the way home from a night out: great hulking boxes that would create a meal out of some bread roll with a bit of chook and gravy. I was amazed. An instant convert.

I think my problem was that I always maintained a belief in the futuristic and miraculous capabilities of microwaves, which, as a friend of mine described, was, 'Very, Redcliffe, very Queensland of you, William.'

While I thought this comment a tad patronising, it was probably quite true.

From cooking boiled, poached and scrambled eggs in the Nuke Box and giving new life to stale bread, pizzas and almost any leftover takeaway, while heating cold coffee and soup to scorched lips and blistered gum levels, I've maintained the faith.

Perhaps too much. I've misguidedly tried to draw on my inner MacGyver and use the Nuke Box to dry clothes, including school uniforms, wet footy boots and soaked slippers. None of it ended well.

I definitely went a MacGyver too far when I thought I could reanimate a mobile phone that'd gone through the wash by blasting it in the Nuke Box. No Lazarus for the long-cycle soggy mobile, just an explosion and some explaining to do to the concierge.

When I told him what I'd done, he said, 'Fair enough.' Maybe he was a fan of MacGyver.

It helps if one's MacGyver is witnessed and appreciated, validated almost, because if you try to tell somebody about it, the MacGyver has a tendency to sound like a tall story, that you are having a lend or telling a furphy. The word 'furphy' derived from the farm water carts manufactured by the Furphy engineering firm of Shepparton. The carts were used to transport water around army camps during World War I and the expression 'a furphy' became a name for the stories that were told and exchanged by the soldiers as they gathered at a cart. Basically, a group of men would sit together and pass the time by bullshitting to each other, or if not exactly bullshitting, they'd add a bit of mayo to a story.

It's the same thing as an Elvis add-on, because the story being told is so improbable, the teller might as well add an Elvis sighting to the story or, even better, make Elvis a central character in the saga.

For example, nobody could quite believe how I got the outdoor spa to the shire tip by myself, but it was a hamburger with lots of MacGyvering.

The spa had come with the house, and I supposed had been there as long as the pool. The pool was lovely, although I was about as much use as a chocolate teapot when it came to maintaining it.

Thankfully, my pool man, called Doctor Pool, saw to that. He came to me as a result of a plea for help after I had tried applying some do-it-yourself remedies. He pulled me aside at a barbecue and asked for a quiet word.

He said he didn't want to embarrass me. 'Everything you could have done to this pool wrong you've done, and then there's a few things I've never thought possible that have been done.'

So, with our relationship established, I said one day that I wasn't keen on the spa. Doctor Pool nodded. 'We should take care of it,' I said. Doctor Pool nodded. I thought this meant he was going to remove it. He thought it meant he should fix it up. He did the latter. I paid the bill and still nobody used the bloody thing. Although my son did turn it on, but had second thoughts when he saw it in action. He thought it looked like the sort of thing that James Bond villains use to see off their incompetent henchmen and underlings.

One morning, I arose and surveyed my domain. The garden had been tidied. I had taken ute-loads of rubbish to the tip. The ute was still there in the front yard. I looked at it. I decided I liked utes.

Not for the first time, I thought that even though I knew the car industry in Australia was extinct — what a good idea it was to let that go bung — I miss utes. Proper ones, not the things that have gone to ute gym and come out looking like a four-wheeled Arnold Schwarzenegger, but those older styles that were the honest yeomanry of working vehicles. And then I had an epiphany — they were the automotive equivalent of Acco Daks. Cars that laid down a challenge, that made you ask yourself, What have I done today? What else can I do today?

Acco Daks utes. It was like Matt Hammond was standing alongside me with his Accordion Trousers, forerunners to Acco Daks. And half the Albany whalers were with him. All standing there, willing one to action.

I looked at that Acco Daks ute. It stood empty, daring adventure. There was still a few hours before it had to be back at the rental from whence it had come. The empty ute seemed to say, 'Come on, have a crack!'

Who was I to ignore the challenge of an Acco Daks ute?

I stood in my PJs, slippers and dressing gown. The spa stood empty, mocking me with its uselessness.

I unplugged the spa and shifted it. Surprisingly, it moved. I levered it up and turned it on its side. A few bits and pieces fell off, but I managed to tumble it along the deck.

I was determined, in cut-snake manner, to achieve what I was attempting without changing my present MacGyver garb. I had got it to the ute when my niece and her then-boyfriend popped in to say hello after a trip to the beach.

'Jimmy,' I said, 'give us a hand.'

The said Jimmy was completing his training to be a surgeon. He was an efficient, precise, capable and logical young man. He had no conception of what I was doing.

'All I need is for you to give a push, I'll do the rest,' I said, as I tripped a little over my errant dressing-gown sash.

Amazingly, I got the spa onto the tray of the ute. It stood teetering on the tray, I put the small sides up. 'That will secure it.'

Jimmy the soon to be surgeon looked at me.

'Are you going to tie it on?'

'No,' I said. 'Its weight will keep it there.'

Jimmy the soon to be surgeon looked at the spa and then at me and said, 'William, you are fucking insane.'

I told him it would make the trip to the tip more epic. He offered to come with me and help but I told him I had to do this on my own. But I added that I couldn't wear my robe. The jammies and slippers were doable but the dressing gown was a bridge too far. 'Why ruin a MacGyver with a bit of showboating?'

He stared and smiled. Then he said solemnly, 'May your journey be fruitful.'

He laughed as I drove off. The spa did everything it could to fall off but, encouraged by me screaming at it to 'Stay there!', it remained onboard. I arrived at the tip and was greeted with an epically disinterested tip attendant.

'I have a spa to dump,' I said, as if I had caught a prize-winning marlin with my bare hands.

She looked at me with bored eyes.

'Spa?' She checked the weight. 'Not a bad effort.'

My chest heaved with pride. I nodded. Then she gave me a command which still puzzles me with its combination of items.

'Spas . . . Spas . . . spas go with the old mattresses.'

Why, I have no idea.

There was one last hurdle or mini mountain to climb: the steep drive up a ramp and then the descent to the mattress graveyard.

When I got to the top, I heard a voice cry out, 'Chucking out a spa, some fucking blokes have too much money!' and looked to see another tip customer unloading his ute.

He was dressed in jeans, an Akka Dakka tank top and was wearing speed dealers. In his free hand he held a can of bourbon and cola.

I took him in.

'Don't worry, mate,' he said. 'I didn't drive. Just helping me mate.'

I took in his mate, a man clad in immaculate tip wear. Overalls, boots, safety glasses and gloves. He nodded at me. I nodded at him. His mate with the bourbon and cola nosed at me. I nodded back and said, 'If you want the spa, you are welcome to it.'

He nodded and said, 'Let's have a look-see.'

I waited in the car for what seemed like an age then decided he must have had second thoughts and I drove off down to where the mattresses lay.

I stopped the car, got out, and heard a whoop.

It was Bourbon and Cola; he'd come down on the back of the ute with the spa.

'Good ride, mate!' he said as I tried to apologise. 'Don't worry, as good as being on a fucking Moomba float!'

He watched me push the spa off the edge and offered the validation of a kindred spirit. 'Big effort with the spa, my man, and extra points for wearing your PJs.' He toasted me with his can of bourbon and cola.

There, a validated MacGyver and not an Elvis in sight.

•

Sometimes you don't need to share a MacGyver, especially when it happens in your castle. 'A man's home is his castle' goes the old saying from a fellow called Sir Edward Coke. It dates to the seventeenth century so you can forgive Ted for being gender specific, but the meaning is: whoever the homeowner may be, they enjoy being the ruler of that home and having the final word on who may enter their domain.

Now, we human beings tend to regard ourselves as the only show in town so it's an adventure when our castle is breached by an unwelcome visitor.

I'm not thinking about the creatures we share the world with, like the various creepy-crawlies that exist within our castles in astonishing numbers. Dust mites, spiders, geckos, ants, fleas and all those other things you pretend aren't really there.

I cordially welcome dogs, can sort of come at cats, and even gave the benefit of the doubt to a friend with a pet white rat which would roam about his apartment in a plastic sphere. My pal swore the rat, named Alvin, was happy but I was never quite sure, although I can remember the night we watched a rugby test together when Alvin rolled into the room and stopped in front of the telly, and happily took in a good few plays, twitching his nose.

These are predictable enough creatures. It's when something gets in the house that has no right being there that life gets a bit interesting. It's never happened to me, but I've heard of people finding snakes in their homes. Like the story that made the BBC news site about an Australian woman being bitten by a snake in the toilet.

Thankfully, the snake was a non-venomous python, but, really, your mind doesn't want to go there. There are countless tales of possums wreaking havoc in the roof and I remember the hysteria of my youth when the family home was breached by that most unwelcome of guests: the cane toad.

We would all start shrieking 'Toad' and my mother would gallantly get her trusty ice-cream container to trap Toady and do whatever she did with the dreadful things.

One night the toad cry went up and my mother turned away white-faced with the fateful words, 'God help me, I'll have to get a bloody bucket.'

I never really handled these visitations from nature well and not much has changed.

The other night just on dusk a bird flew in through the bank of French doors I had open.

It was a tiny wren and petrified, and I was a large middle-aged battleship of a man and fairly unhinged. Call it what you will, carrying on like a pork chop, being as silly as a wheel and, probably most appropriately, I was behaving like a galah.

'Get out!' I said to the birdie. 'Get, you bloody thing!'

It flew about for a seeming eternity while I roared, 'No, no, not that way!'

Somewhere, in some part of my brain, I knew that speaking, or in my case yelling, at the bird wasn't going to do any good. But it made me feel like I was achieving something.

Eventually I calmed down enough to type into a search engine 'how do you get a bird out of a room?'

'Confine the area, switch off all lights and open the nearest window.'

Seeing the bank of French doors was open I ticked that off. I got up to close doors to other parts of my castle. The bird whizzed past and landed on a full-sized cutout of Dean Martin I happen to own. (It was a present and every home or castle should have one.) Deano didn't seem to care; his handsome head was tilted back and he was smiling. He hadn't had this good a time since the Rat Pack were the kings of Vegas.

I switched off the lights. Interesting. It was dark by now and I couldn't see a thing. I tried to reason with the bird and attempted to modulate my tones.

'Come on,' I said in my most soothing manner. 'Out you go.' The bird flew about, I yelled, 'You bastard. You rotten bastard!' and, crouching, made for the doors where I crashed into a set of golf clubs I had used earlier in the day and had helpfully left there. I said some magic words. Golf clubs seem to bring that out in me – that and castle invaders.

I stood up and the bird flew past my ear. More magic words. I switched the light on and the birdie had left my castle.

I noticed it had left a deposit as a memento of its visit. At least it didn't poo on Deano. He was smiling. I laughed.

I'd like to think the wren was happy too, but it's a little humbling thinking how disturbing a bit of nature can be in your castle.

Outside, it's another thing, and this is where a certain honest assessment of one's character needs to be made.

Whether or not you have what it takes to be what is termed 'a good old Australian smart-arse'. This is not necessarily a bad thing. But it can be annoying to others.

I was talking wildlife the other day with a neighbour who was in the process of building a shed in his backyard and had popped his head over the fence to apologise for some of the magic words he'd uttered during his labours.

I assured him it was all quite tame. He nodded, saying he didn't think I would've minded but thought he should be polite. I've been known to use not just colourful language but high-definition techno-colourful language, especially when I am trying to do something around the house.

Some bees had made a hive in the roof of a bungalow further around the neighbour's yard and this started the wildlife chat.

Why is it that the last month of summer seems to be a busier time than usual for creature sightings and meetings? Perhaps it's the last gasp of activity, or because it's the time when holidays are ending and real life begins again, so you tend to notice things like creepy-crawlies more.

The bees were an example. The neighbour had tried to get rid of the things humanely for most of the summer, attempting deterrents such as bombarding the surrounds of the hive with strategically placed mothballs, even sonic weapons were attempted on one priceless weekend. Two speakers were placed on the roof and a collection of appalling sounds howled into the hive.

'The bloody things didn't even move, just enjoyed a bee dance party. Beehive 54,' said my neighbour, who'd brought over a bottle of wine to apologise for the sonic bee-wrangling experiment. 'The internet really is full of crap ideas sometimes.'

I asked him if it was the internet's idea to play Bee Gees and ABBA as well as the doof doof music.

'No,' said my neighbour. 'That was me. Showing my vintage, I'm afraid.'

The bees buzzed about the shed, and we watched for a moment. They seemed to be frantic, making the most of the time before a pest man came to remove them, for the neighbour had run out of useful tips from 'the internet'.

'Seems a shame, really, they don't seem to be doing anybody any harm, but I should do something I suppose – I just don't like the idea of sprays and chemicals.'

It's strange the way almost all the insects we humans come into contact with are something to be sprayed or squashed or swatted away, something identified as a threat to us.

Mozzies and flies I completely get, but there's lots of casualties out there that are basically guilty by association.

Take spiders. Of course, there's threatening nasties like the trapdoor, funnel web or redback but, by and large, huntsmen and daddy-long-legs are basically insect deterrents in themselves. Yet most of us remove, flatten or exterminate household spiders.

The variety of beetles and bugs at the end of summer is also stupendous. Surely they can't all be bad for you? I remember an old shirt box of my father's that my mother had padded out with cotton wool, upon which she had placed a collection of deceased beetles and bugs. It was a little bit like a rectangular Tomb of Kings with the shiny little ex-creatures lying in state and stark against the snowy white of the cotton wool. A Christmas beetle shone gold, shimmering there on the white clouds. I thought them incredible as a child and it was always a treat to hold the box and look at the assembled colours and formations, things of beauty in the Pelaco frame.

As we become more urbanised and live in a set and controlled existence, the other-worldliness of creepy-crawlies seems crazier by the day. Aliens intruding into our spaces that must be eradicated at all costs. Perhaps the fear of small creatures is hardwired into us from threats posed by centuries of plague, disease and even superstition. Some bugs are filthy, unpleasant and a threat. But more insects are becoming recognised as a source of coin and nutrition – crickets, worms, roaches – and more are being cured, dried, barbecued, roasted and broiled to tempt the human palate.

And bees? Beside the honey they produce they're vital to the health of our ecology. They pollinate plants and make the world a better place for birds and humans.

I woke up one morning not long after the Beehive 54 disco effort and it was much like the beginning of any other day. I got up, donned my preferred garment of endeavour — a dressing gown — and mooched around the kitchen.

It was here I noticed two things. One was a paper note with the WiFi details and password. I had written this out for the Gazelle and had meant to leave it in my little writing shed by the side of the house.

The Gazelle was the name I'd given to a friend who was a sports journalist. His movements were so low and glacial that the name was bestowed upon him by colleagues from the press box, especially when the only time he moved with any speed was to the lunch tables at the MCG.

He was in my little shed doing a golfing podcast. I had meant to put the password info on the door last night, so I went to do it now.

The second thing I noticed was a bee. Bees.

There were three or four of them buzzing in the kitchen. They left when I opened a side door. I thought nothing of it. Things were always getting into the castle: wrens, of course, and even microbats would slip in and scream around and then find their way out again, so bees were the least of my worries.

Until I went down to my shed. I opened the door to find the Gazelle nodding at me. It gave me a start and I screamed.

He screamed. We all screamed. I wondered how it sounded on his podcast.

I continued to scream, he stopped, and he mouthed a silent 'Fuck'. He pointed. I immediately checked my dressing gown, thinking perhaps my vitals were showing. No, all good.

I turned and followed his finger; he said something in a measured tone about someone's form on the Asian tour. The Gazelle was nothing if not unflappable. He continued droning on about the tour and going about his podcast as I looked up to see a dark cloud of bees swirling around above the roof of the bungalow next door.

I walked over to the fence and peered over. There were two figures dressed in outfits that looked like something from a science fiction film I remember with Dustin Hoffman in it, *Outbreak*. Although the film costumes were yellow and sort of fitted. These were baggy, fluffy things. One figure was very tall and the other, the one that was closer to me, was very short. The little one reminded me of a kid going off to school in a new blazer or uniform that was about four sizes too large, something they would grow into.

Whoever was in that suit had enough room to put in a pool and spa.

I waved. He turned and walked over slowly, though the suit was so baggy it seemed to take a while to determine which way he was headed. He looked like a big, poorly baked meringue.

He spoke through a gauze mask.

'Have. You. Been. Stung?' he said slowly. It sounded like the Gazelle on his podcast.

I was about to say no but then he said it again in the same steady almost pedantic manner. 'Have. You. Any. Ice? Stay calm. Stay calm.'

He sounded like a cross between the robot from *Lost in Space* and Leslie Nielsen from *The Naked Gun*. He sounded serious, but the well-modulated almost voice-over man manner had a hint of taking the piss a bit.

He must have assumed that I had been stung by the way I'd screamed when I saw the Gazelle. And by my appearance. Fresh from the cot with my epic bedhead and puffy eyes.

I decided to have a bit of fun. I puffed out my cheeks. 'I don't know,' I croaked. 'I feel funny.'

'Breathe . . . slowly . . . Slowly,' the little shape-shifting meringue said.

I remembered Doctor Smith, the howling theatrical offsider of the robot in *Lost in Space* and how he would whine his catchphrase. I followed suit.

'Oh, the pain . . . the pain.'

And I ducked down behind the fence.

The shape-shifting meringue stopped with the well-modulated tones and sounded like Yobbo Ahab when he had missed the bus to Sandgate.

'Fuck! Dave! It's happened again! 'Nother punter's been stung!'

Then I popped back up, loomed over the fence at him, giggled and said, 'No, mate, all good. That's the sort of talent that gets two Logies.'

The shape-shifting meringue seethed and said slowly, 'So, you're a funny fella, champ.'

I laughed again. He'd champed me, the international sign that someone thinks you are a smart-arse.

'Have my moments.' And this is one of them, I thought to myself. 'Few bees about,' I said helpfully.

The shape-shifting meringue was definitely in *Naked Gun* territory. 'You think?' he said dryly. 'Yes, a few more than we thought.'

'How many you reckon?'

Now the meringue sounded professional again. 'Well, I'd say forty thousand.'

'Must have taken you a while to count them.'

This time he seethed with a capital S. 'Yes, chief, you are a funny fella.'

Chief! Gold-plated smart-arse.

The meringue told me that they had set up a draw hive and that the bees would eventually settle down and go there. He told me to shut my windows, and everything should be fine. And then he shape-shifted off.

I said, 'Okay,' turned around and promptly got stung a couple of times.

•

Most piss-taking is spontaneous. You don't think that much about what you are going to do. And it is slightly less angular than being a smart-arse. A sense of fun, rather than just being a pest.

If there is a patron saint of piss-taking, it has to be the bloke on the penny-farthing from Redcliffe.

During one of the interminable Melbourne lockdowns, the Queensland State Archives released a series of small films online, some of them little more than clips, about all things Queensland. I was alerted to one by PB. 'Brother, you must watch this. Jump in the old DeLorean and go back to 1979.'

I clicked on the link. Perhaps it was just because it was a grey old lockdown day, but as soon as I saw the view of that water my heart leapt a little. It was like recognising an old friend: the long and bumpy bridge.

The film was without sound and was, I think, a mixture of news coverage of the opening of the Houghton Highway, the new roadway that stretched across Hays Inlet and the banks of mangroves that lined the shore. It was replacing the old Hornibrook Highway, always boasted about in the strangest terms to all who went to primary school on the peninsula. 'The longest unbroken bit of roadway in the Southern Hemisphere.'

I could almost feel the car lurching over the rickety Hornibrook, it felt like a comfortable sideshow alley ride at the Ekka, the Brisbane Agricultural Show. We all thought the new Houghton Highway was a spanking bit of infrastructure that was sleek and modern and the perfect gift for the twentieth anniversary of Redcliffe becoming a city. But after its opening the Hornibrook was closed to traffic and so the time it took to cross the bay was just as long.

And the new bridge was terrible to drive across. Instead of the gentle up and over bumps, the whole car rattled and shook over the bumpy surface.

My father and mother called driving across the Houghton Highway a dose of the 'Aznavours' because they said the effect of the bumpy ride made your voice sound like the wavering vibrato of the French singer Charles Aznavour. It got downstreamed to 'Let's Dance' as you drove over the bridge because of the French warbler's hit 'Dance the Old-Fashioned Way'.

All that was in the future though: the soundless film was only concerned with the pageantry of the peninsula on the day the bridge opened. It was on a Thursday, but it was school holidays. I had a four-hour shift at the Coles down by the jetty, $8.80 pay and I remember I bought a discounted, meaning heavily scratched, ELO Greatest Hits album for $7.99 that my mother thought a waste of money. 'Listening to that silly man with all that hair, is it supposed to jump about like that?' she boomed.

True, the songs did have that self-sampled feel to them, but I put my mother's dismissive tone down to the effects of the bridge opening. My mum and my sister went. As a part of the grand opening, you could walk along the length of the new bridge, which was a novel idea, but the only way to get back to where you started was to walk back the entire length.

'Whose bright idea was that? Grand opening? Foot-falconing for over an hour isn't a grand anything. Just a long way to walk,' said my mother.

Watching the video, I hadn't realised at the time there were so many marching girls in their funny biscuit-tin outfits. Some looked like they were dressed as air stewards, or stewardesses as they would have been called then. Funny peaked caps, or things that looked like they were knock-offs of the creations that the guards at Buckingham Palace wore. Pleated skirts rippled as gloved hands swished past and they marched in step past the Eventide Nursing Home.

Nurses stood on tiptoe, peering over the fence to view young girls in funny martial-cum-ballet uniforms stride along, shepherded by middle-aged mothers in billowing sun dresses and bad sunnies.

Later in the film you could see the effects of foot-falconing on the marching girls. There was a decided lack of interest in keeping step and some of the hats seemed to be at alarming angles.

There were pipe bands in kilts, with a bloke I remembered who worked at the timber mill up near the showgrounds. I could tell it was him by his bow-legged gait.

There was the Humpybong drum and fife band, and the city band. Some of the schools had students make a special effort to show up in uniform. The idea was that people would walk across and meet halfway. But that all went south in a hurry and any semblance of order soon vanished. The whole event became a muddled free-for-all after the dignitaries, boy scouts, marching girls, vintage car enthusiasts, fife bands, Scottish pipe bands, the odd happy dog and people from next door and down the street swarmed onto the new bridge.

The scouts appeared and were formed like a police line-up, with a few looking decidedly uncomfortable, and on the other side were some of the air cadets who looked like they were up against a firing squad wall.

It's a good thing some people were dressed up because most of the other people present were dressed in Redcliffe tuxedos — meaning they were bare-chested. If they were wearing a shirt it was of the T variety. If some of the Albany whalers had been there, they wouldn't have been out of place. It seemed that if people wanted to get dressed up back then, they wore long socks.

It was heart-warming and familiar. When I showed my kids, they both laughed and said that not much had changed in Redcliffe sartorially since 1979. It was true, people still wear the same clobber today.

Except safari suits. The mayor, Ray Frawley, one of life's great blokes, had one on, complete with a lapel full of badges. Back then they were the other suits, worn by men like Joh Bjelke-Petersen, the long-time Queensland premier; Jim Houghton, the Speaker of the House, after whom the bridge was named; and one of the great characters of Queensland politics in the Bjelke-Petersen era, the Minister for Everything, Russ Hinze, who, after decades of public service, came undone by way of the Fitzgerald Inquiry.

'A right crook, but not a bad bloke,' was my father's assessment. 'At least he gets things done.'

Russ wasn't so much a colourful racing identity as a technocolourful racing identity.

Those 'dignitaries' all arrived in swollen cars like Ford LTDs and Holden Statesmen. The effect was to make them look like heads of crime families from *The Godfather*, especially when there were shots of grim-looking drivers in equally bad suits and dark sunnies leaning on the bonnets of the cars.

There was a hint of skulduggery about them all. Hinze and Houghton had both tried to roll Joh, who had somehow fended them off and become the long-term don. It was a moment in time, and they were at their zenith.

I looked at Hinze, glowering good-naturedly as he sat in a chair that was provided for the dignitaries. He'd always seemed so old to me back then – all that government had – and even now as I looked at his image I thought, you old bugger.

I stopped the film and looked him up. He had been sixty, only a few years older than me now. I looked back at the screen, at Russ Hinze smiling slyly out at me.

I don't know who it was, but someone said that photos, and I suppose films, mean more and say more about the person looking at them than the subjects in the images.

We have the knowledge and know the outcomes, the disgrace that would come, but on this grey morning I looked and thought, we are nearly the same age now and I realised then that I was surprised by the film. Old Russ smiling at a nearly as old William.

There were vintage cars lurching past straggling marching girls and people foot-falconing along the bridge, and amid all this I see him.

Only for an instant. The piss-taker. There is a man, probably around mid-twenties, and he is dressed informally – Stubbies shorts, a short-sleeved shirt with a packet of durries in the breast pocket, thongs on his feet and a hint of mo on his upper lip. A little smile on his face.

And he is riding a giant penny-farthing bicycle.

It is, quite frankly, a moment of brilliant madness. Where did he get it from? Why did he ride it across the bridge? Did he just keep it in his garage, or perhaps on the verandah, and think he'd take it out for a trundle on the big day across the bridge? How far did he have to ride it to get there? And how far did he have to ride it back?

That bike seat would have been hard to ride, especially clothed in only Stubbies.

The whalers would have approved.

It was such an incongruous sight amid the attempted pageantry that I couldn't stop laughing. I played it back and still couldn't quite believe it. Mad bugger. The Penny-Farthing Man of the Peninsula, patron saint of those who take the piss.

CHAPTER 9

MEN OF THEIR TIME

Would you have a beer with LBJ? The 36th President of the United States of America. Lyndon Baines Johnson? I know I would definitely have one with Ian Chappell, former Australian cricket captain. But LBJ? Of all the lists that PB sent me during the coalface years of Covid lockdowns, the one that stumped me was based around an often heard bit of Australian vernacular: 'A good bloke.'

Actually, PB's list was of ten blokes, living or dead, with whom he'd like to have a beer. I just made the assumption that the frothy sharers would be good blokes. Why anybody would want to have a beer with a bad bloke is a bit bewildering but there is really no accounting for people's tastes.

I've had beers with people who I either thought, or had been told, were good blokes, who turned out to be just people.

And some who turned out to be rank flogs. And some who were good blokes.

What's the definition of a good bloke? Somebody who is good company, good-humoured and will lend a hand when it's needed. Someone who doesn't take themselves too seriously but is serious in the work they do when it counts. You don't have to change the world or make it stand on its head.

Everybody has parts of their lives that they are not that proud of, but a one-name famous person, like Winston (as in Churchill) would have a grander sweep to theirs than a one-named person like William (as in McInnes).

Winston would have a torturous relationship with his decision to invade the Dardanelles in World War I, an event which haunted him for the rest of his life. Cue suitable swelling music, probably Elgar or perhaps Walton.

William would have flashbacks of his momentous decision to wear a skivvy, Stubbies and thongs to a party in a late '80s Sydney harbourside location. And his attempts there to 'crack on' to a young woman who helpfully pointed out, during a lull in the party noise, that he had no chance to 'chat her up'. I, William, summoned my inner Churchillian turn of phrase and came up with words that would echo through the ages, 'Awww, come on.'

This did not sway her in any way. She continued to observe that not only was my skivvy – and I remember her bursting out laughing incredulously at the word skivvy and repeating, 'A skivvvvvy!' which sure attracted a good deal of attention from other partygoers – not only was my skivvy dirty, which was quite true, there had been an incident with some tomato sauce outside, but it was adorned with 'Some weird as shit sticker'. This I was unaware of. It turned out to be a Masters of the Universe sticker – an animated comic book fantasy series. These days it has a cult following but back in the party days it was slightly pathetic to see a large man in a sky-blue skivvy wearing a neatly pressed sticker featuring two major Masters of the Universe characters – He-Man, a large muscular fellow in a blond basin-cut mullet and leather nappies holding a sword; and Skeletor, a large muscular blue skeleton (can you have a muscular skeleton? In Masters of the Universe you can!) holding a big sword – grimacing at each other.

To be fair, a friend of mine had found this sticker on a table at the party and, without my knowledge, placed it neatly on my back.

When my delightful quarry pointed out the 'Weird as shit sticker' on my back I tried to turn around to find it. In the process, I dropped my drink and bumped into another partygoer, who in turn spilt his wine over himself and the rest of my skivvy.

All this with a swelling soundtrack of Bonnie Tyler singing 'Holding Out for a Hero'.

For the rest of the night I had to try to evade a small red-headed man with a waxed moustache who wanted to talk about He-Man's adventures. 'I am madly in love with

He-Man, man!' was his constant cry when he saw me drifting back to the beer fridge.

Let's see one-name Winston top that.

A delightful coda to this tortured scene from my past is that, years later, I walked into a studio to start rehearsals on a play and one of my castmates greeted me with 'Hello there, He-Man, where's your skivvy?' This was the woman who I had attempted to impress at the party. We fell about laughing.

Besides the Dardanelles, Churchill was a drinker, prone to depression and a racial imperialist. Other great men of history were just as epically flawed. JFK was a womanising man of epic ill-health propped up by medication, and Gandhi had a collection of questionable personal habits and uncomfortable characteristics.

A good bloke is probably a more mundane form of being. A feeling you get from someone, of decency and dependability. Basically, to be a good bloke is to be a good man. But then, what's a good man?

And LBJ? Really?

To some, a bloke isn't gender specific. Women can be mates and good blokes. Mates, yes by all means, my anti-skivvy target from the party, for example, is a grand mate. But blokes? I think it's pretty gender specific.

'Sheila' is the female equivalent of bloke, as are 'chicks', 'birds' and 'girls'. While all these terms were probably bestowed upon women by men, over time they have been appropriated by women as terms of empowerment. So, one woman can refer to another woman as an 'awesome chick'.

I still have a tendency to think that calling someone a chick is slightly derogatory, but friends who really are awesome chicks assure me that in the right context it is fine.

The last time I heard anybody referring to women as sheilas was when the former British PM David Cameron quoted the former Australian PM Julia Gillard after he thanked her for hosting a Commonwealth Heads of Government conference where it was determined the line of succession for the British Royal Crown would no longer be gender specific, meaning the first-born of the monarch's family would become the heir to the throne, regardless of the person's sex.

Julia Gillard, according to David Cameron, replied to his thanks by saying, 'No worries, David, it's a win for sheilas everywhere.'

There seems to be a hint of irony in using 'sheila' now, as if it has become a bit archaic and has a comic effect when it is applied in conversation. So Julia Gillard celebrated an apparently modernising decision of the monarchy while also poking fun by using a term the English thought applied only to common women, not those of royal birth.

Certainly, there are awesome chicks and top sheilas I would gladly have a sip with.

Take the mother at high school who thought I was the boy who had just been 'dumped' by her daughter. I'd asked for a salad roll, but this lovely woman basically gave me a Christmas hamper with the words, 'Don't worry, love, there'll be others!'

When I told her she'd mixed me up with another student, she smiled and said, 'Well, someone will break your heart one day, so enjoy!'

Or the gang I was a part of when I volunteered to work in the canteen of my son's school and found myself to be the only father present. I enjoyed the chat and the company but became a little perplexed when a certain stillness came over the canteen as the recess bell rang.

I turned to a mother next to me and she said, 'Time to put your game face on, Big Fella, here they come.'

We laughed.

But the bell was like a bellowing horn sounding the call to attack, and what descended upon us was a horde of fourteen-year-old boys who had to be fought off as if they were marauding Vikings.

'Make sure they don't take your hands with them!' another mother said.

There's also the mother of an acting chum who wouldn't stop waving from her seat in the theatre until her son waved back from the stage. Pretending to be Shakespearean knights going off to battle, I saw him wave a little while Harry the King was banging on.

'Mum in tonight?'

'Yes,' he whispered with his other hand holding a huge sword. 'Fourth row, smack in the middle.'

And we assembled knights, and King Harry, all waved with our free hand.

For quite a few Saturdays I had the misfortune to be on the shot-put pit at Little Athletics, and the mother of one kid used to drive me insane.

Every Saturday she'd be at me to check if the figures were right, if there were fouls or infractions by the nine-year-old 'competitors'.

On the last Saturday of the season, she approached, I drew a breath, and she gave me a box of choccies and a hug. 'For helping out and being a nice man.'

I nearly cried.

Another awesome chick. But for argument's sake, not a bloke.

I doubt any of those women would like to be referred to as blokes.

Sometimes one of those big single-name historical figures can attain good bloke status if they rub the right shoulders. Take Gough Whitlam when he met Vincent Lingiari in 1975.

Whitlam met Vincent Lingiari at Daguragu, formerly known as Wattie Creek, in the Northern Territory to hand over the deeds of the land to the Gurindji people, nine years after they walked off the Wave Hill cattle station owned by the multinational Vestey corporation.

Lingiari was the head stockman at the Wave Hill Station but received no pay for his position for many years. He received food and tobacco and occasionally five pounds in pocket money, but no wage, no acknowledgement of his position of authority. He was a quiet man who was a leader not only in his workplace but also amongst his people he was elder in law.

A man whose actions spoke as grandly as the finest orator's words.

He never belittled or personally attacked the bosses of the cattle stations, but one morning he simply said that he had had enough of his people being treated 'like dogs' in their own land and he walked off the job to lead a strike that lasted nine years, one of the longest-running industrial actions in Australia.

Simply taking industrial action is not always necessarily a noble act, but Lingiari and his people's act of standing up for civil, industrial and land rights is unlike many overt acts of valour. No showboating, no mayo added, no loud voices but sure ones.

It was the quiet dignity, unassuming courage, and a sure belief in the basic rightness of what they were doing which is so moving and remarkable. For nine years he led the action, becoming a focal point for land rights and perhaps it was fitting that his timeless and patient authority was matched with one of the most ramshackle but glorious shooting stars of Australian public life, the Whitlam Government.

It was Andrew Denton, the Australian journalist, who said that BG and AG stand for Before Gough and After Gough, for Australia was never the same. Whitlam was transformative and chaotic and exciting, but he never shone so bright as he did with Lingiari under the outback sun.

Photographer Mervyn Bishop had Lingiari and Whitlam recreate the moment of handing over the title of the lands and the image he captured would lift the heart of anyone who cares to think about a fair go and generosity.

Whitlam stooped from his great height and swept a handful of soil in his big hand, then poured the soil into Vincent Lingiari's hands.

The grand eloquence of Gough was on full display that day.

'Vincent Lingiari, I solemnly hand to you these deeds as proof, in Australian law, that these lands belong to the Gurindji people, and I put into your hands part of the earth itself as a sign that this land will be the possession of you and your children forever.'

Then came the words of a good bloke: 'Let us live happily together as mates, let us not make it hard for each other . . . We want to live in a better way together, Aboriginals and white men, let us not fight over anything, let us be mates.'

Visionary eloquence met with quiet dignity and humility.

It's not a stretch to say that Lingiari and Whitlam achieved gold-level good bloke status that day.

•

Good blokes? I like to think two unnamed Australians who went out to cast a line would count as a practical definition of what that phrase might mean.

Hieu Van Le, former Governor of South Australia, once gave a speech about his arrival on a boat one early morning into Darwin Harbour.

Groups of families stared ahead through the humid, misty haze of a Territory wet season with a mixture of fear, apprehension and doubt.

They heard voices approaching. And a motor.

Some on board the boat began to cry. Some said it was the security services. They would be interned. Locked up. Turned away, maybe; some thought they would be shot.

Out of the mist came a tinny. On board were two enormous Australian men, fishing rods in one hand, cans of beer in the other.

The Vietnamese refugees stared as the little tinny, sinking low in the water, came closer until it was almost touching the refugee boat.

Then the men in the tinny lifted their beers and said with a laugh, 'G'day there. Welcome to Australia.'

'I cannot tell you what that moment was for me,' Hieu Van Le says, 'when I met my first Australians, I cannot tell you how much that moment means to me now, that such generosity and friendship was given to us. And I can never explain how proud I am to be Australian and how thankful I am to this wonderful country.'

Thanks should be given to Hieu Van Le for gracing us with his presence. I'm sure the two unknown good blokes in the tinny would be the first to recognise a fellow member of the good bloke tribe.

•

I think of my father's words about Russ Hinze. 'A right crook but not a bad bloke, he gets things done.'

When Russ Hinze died, few shed a tear for him. He was such an obvious example of the depth of the corruption that had eaten away at due process and good government in Queensland.

It's hard today to grasp just how thoroughly Johannes Bjelke-Petersen and his National Party dominated the state of Queensland during the 1970s and 1980s. He seemed omnipresent. His victory in the 1974 election decimated the Labor Party to a cricket team of eleven sitting members.

Tommy Burns was an old Labor warrior from Queensland who played a pivotal role in the modernisation of the Federal Labor Party in the late 1960s and early 1970s. He was instrumental in the election of Gough Whitlam's Labor Government in 1972 and in 1974 it was his task to pick up the scraps of what was left of Labor in Queensland, the cricket team, and try to fashion it into some kind of functioning political unit.

He came from the other end of Moreton Bay to us at Redcliffe, sprouting from Wynnum and the Redlands area. He was known to my dad as the sort of bloke you'd want on your side, but 'By Christ he was a cranky bugger. He'd pick a fight with his own shadow to prove a point.'

My dad also said that Burns was one of the most honest men he'd met in Labor. 'When he says he'd back you up he never, never left your side. Mad as a two-bob watch but a good bloke.'

Burns was mad about fishing and had a tinny that he called *The Electorate* so when he wanted to skive off and throw a line, or perhaps tend his oyster racks, away he'd go and callers to his office, be they fellow politicians, constituents, lobbyists, or journalists, were always told that Mr Burns was unavailable as he was out in the electorate. He had my dad's nod of being a good bloke, but he proved it when Russ Hinze died.

In 1993 Burns said, 'I am a larrikin; I like doing my own thing. I like telling a bastard he's a bastard because he is a bastard.'

He was also true to his word – he said he would never attend Joh Bjelke-Petersen's funeral because of all Joh's alleged crimes. It was Joh's perceived dishonesty that Burns detested the most and he kept his word; he didn't attend.

Russ Hinze was a different matter. Burns was deputy premier at the time of Hinze's death and spoke about Hinze during a motion of condolence. Hinze had been up to his neck in the mire of the Bjelke-Petersen regime and had few friends at the end of his life and almost none after his death. Except one.

Tom Burns had been told that it was best if his remarks were made in the same manner as the rest of the representatives' words. Tepid and polite. This was probably a mistake.

These were his first words.

'I join with the Premier in offering my condolences to the family of Russ Hinze and to give old Russ a send-off. In many ways, he was one of the great characters of this place. Russ and I had many fights, some of them bitter. But I liked the old bastard. I cannot say it any other way. I am sure that he would appreciate my saying it that way.'

What followed was a litany of arguments over a few beers, celebrations at Christmas parties where Hinze would sing epically out of tune songs, then Hinze growling at Burns like an angry bear when Hinze had to come back from a 'ministerial' trip to Kentucky and the Caribbean when Tom Burns had kicked up a stink just because he could. Hinze also shook his head at Burns' dogged pursuit of what he saw as corruption and inappropriate government. But that didn't mean people couldn't be mates. How could you not be fond of somebody who, when a measure was proposed by a government member that dingos should be castrated because they had been killing sheep on rural properties, replied, 'What good will that do? The dingos are killing the sheep, not fucking them.'

Burns stood in the House and said, 'I come from a school that says that you do not kick a man when he is down, you do not attack a man after he dies, and you do not try to score off his death. I am not trying to score off Russ by saying some of these things today; I am just trying to recall some of the times that we had and a bit of the fun that was associated with them.'

To Burns, the important thing was that when Hinze gave his word, he did his best to keep it. With such an overwhelming majority, the Bjelke-Petersen Government had no need to even deal with the Opposition. But there was one minister who would try. The fact that he was the minister for everything was beneficial. If he thought there was some politicking going on, he would stare down the Opposition when they went calling on ministerial favours but if Hinze thought the Opposition members were really trying to do something for often neglected electorates, he would try to help.

'In those days, he was the only Minister who, if one went to him and asked him to do something, he would try to do something. On many occasions after we left other Ministers, they would say that they would get their advisers to look into the matter, and we would know that that meant we had lost. Russo never acted like that. He was fair dinkum in that way.'

Burns' voice became shaky when he finished his speech. 'I have called him an old crook to his face all his life. I do not withdraw those remarks about him at all, and I am sure that he would not want me to do so. But I always said that he was a good bloke, and if I had to have a fight somewhere I would rather have a bloke like him behind me than some of the others I've come across. I am sorry to see him go, and I am sorry about the way he went.'

I thought of Russ Hinze and Tom Burns when I crossed the bridge to Redcliffe recently. Russ Hinze smiling out from the old footage of the highway opening. Then I looked out across the bay, and I remember reading a report of Tom Burns's death, an apparent heart attack on his houseboat near his oyster lease in Moreton Bay.

He was out in the electorate.

•

I was going back to Redcliffe in part to catch up with my family and PB, maybe talk about that list of beer participants.

I was staying at a new apartment complex just across the road from Margate Beach. It was on the site of an old mower shop that had displayed the mowers on the wraparound verandah as if they were residents sunning themselves on the deck and taking in the view of the bay.

Before that, it had been a rather bleak boarding house. It had seemed much happier as a home for Victas and Rovers.

I got out of the car and flinched in the heat, even though it was late July, almost time for a Queensland winter to begin. I was about to grumble a little when I turned to see a grown man, perhaps in his early to mid-thirties, standing in the middle of the street. He was dressed in denim shorts and an orange singlet with the words 'Beach Boy' written across the chest. He was wearing black runners and talking rather animatedly to the street. He was, in fact, commentating. Saying names. He was, as my mum might have said, not quite right. But she would add, whoever really is?

He had two sticks, one in each hand. With his right hand, he tried to flick the stick from his left hand over the power lines above. He had a shouty voice. 'It's Graeme Hughes,' – Graeme Hughes? He hadn't commentated for over thirty years – 'live from Leichhardt Oval and we've Rod Wishart, the dead-eye from the Illawarra, Moreton Steelers . . . 49ers . . . Dolphins . . . the Dolphins. THE DOLPHINS . . . attempting to get the ball between the lines from the side . . . bit . . . line . . . The SIDELINE! And here he goes, and it looks good . . .'

He flicked the stick in the air and got it three-quarters of the way to the power lines before it tumbled down and hit him. On his head.

He flinched, but only slightly, and then he was back to Leichhardt Oval in another universe.

'It looked good but . . . missed, but no, the touch judge's call! One down and one flag UP! It's there!'

And this bloke, Beach Boy, stood to attention in the middle of the street, holding the stick up in the air with his outstretched arm like a touch judge.

He looked unaccountably happy with himself and Rod Wishart, who hadn't pulled on a football boot in over twenty years.

An old man in the garden across the street said warmly, 'Well done, him. He got the extras!'

The Beach Boy waved his stick to the old man, and to the street, then walked into a nearby house.

I caught a lungful of sea air from the waters of Moreton Bay and I looked at the old man. He checked me out and said, almost protectively, 'He's kicking, or whatever it is he's doing, very well today.'

He was talking about Beach Boy, his neighbour from across the street.

'He is,' I heard myself say. I forgot about the heat and looked at the old man, smiled.

The old man gave me a little wave and a nod of his head. What a good bloke.

It's rather lovely to be back in Redcliffe.

Good blokes.

•

Later that day, I catch up with PB and he is eager to share his newest brew, a Russian stout he named after himself. He presents it with pride. I ask if it really is a Russian stout. He says he simply made it in a rush because he had to be somewhere else and ran out of time. 'But the thing tastes great. It shouldn't, but it does. So, made in a rush, thrown together and it turns out a treat so it's a Russian stout.'

Fair enough. We open it and sip, and it tastes . . . like it was made in a rush. I say this to PB, and he bobbles his head. Clutch-Cargos a bit and he calls me a goose.

I sip again and tell him it tastes . . . not too bad.

Then we talk about his list. He loves lists. He asks if I do. I stare at him.

'Come on,' he says. 'What is not to like?'

I think about lists.

At the beginning of high school one of our teachers encouraged us all to make a list of things we wanted to achieve during the course of the year. I can't remember anything on the list I made and so I can't remember whether anything was achieved. The story of my life.

Lists? Never been too enthusiastic about them and I admitted this to a uni lecturer after he'd questioned a certain lack of organisational detail in my work methods. Meaning, of course, I was enjoying myself way too much at the students' club. He was a fellow traveller of the high school teacher and encouraged me to invest some of my time in making lists of academic goals to assist in the timely completion of my work.

I told him I preferred a more free-range work method; he told me I was 'frightened' of lists.

His view was along the lines of life being 'temporal'. We all have a use-by date and lists smack of trying to control life, which is a finite thing. Lists may ease people's anxiety and make order out of the chaos, but ultimately lists are an artificial construct. 'You see that construct, but don't have the courage to commit against eternity.'

This sort of stuff from a bloke with a bushranger beard and a Midnight Oil t-shirt who was in charge of a Humanities elective.

An old footy coach also extolled the benefits of a list to me. 'It gives you guidance and direction and goals in life.'

They all might have had a point because I always vow to make a list of what I want for my next shopping trip, instead of just meandering aimlessly in the aisles picking up things I fancy.

Many people love lists and not just the ones they make themselves. Lists abound on websites, social media, in magazines. Lists about things to do, places to be, things to see. Celebrities, reality TV stars, restaurants, cars, dogs, coffee shops, on and on. And then lists on what the lists say about you.

Oddly there's never lists about the ten best bus stops, railway stations, tram routes, public toilets, or carparks. Things that people would actually use.

My friend told me she found a list made by her late dad. He'd written it years ago, after he'd retired from a hugely rich and successful career. Three entries. 'Sort out shed. Sort out finances. Sort out MYSELF.'

This bloke had lived a wonderful life. Yet in the time he had left he wanted to sort himself out. I found that incredibly moving. I hope he got there, or maybe making the list was enough.

Funny old things, lists.

I look at my old friend.

PB looks at me.

He says that, on another day, he might choose ten different

blokes to have a beer with, but then he thinks he may not. Anyway, he says as his head bobbles a bit, it's just a silly list.

'LBJ?' I say.

PB sighs, sips, and says, 'Look at the list. It should be self-explanatory.'

I open my phone and peruse his list.

1. Paul Keating: His views on anything and everything would make interesting listening, plus you'd feel safe in his cabal!

2. Robert Mitchum: In the first age of 'celebrity cool', when most confected 'cool' rather than displayed it, he was the embodiment of one cool fucker. Plus, anyone who can snap their fingers as loudly as he did in *Cape Fear* would surely garner the attention of even the most reluctant waitstaff!

3. Shane Warne: Such an unaffected bloke who saw life as one big pantomime and behaved accordingly.

4. LBJ: A man who tried to end poverty in his country, to spread equality and opportunity. And a man who pursued a war of such folly for pride. But for his own or his nation's? A bloke of extremes. And anyone who can use the term 'ball room' on a White House telephone and not be referring to a gala function or a debutante is worthy of sharing a beer with!

5. The Natufian, Egyptian or Turk who first inadvertently left wet bread and malt to warm and ferment and drank the result.

6. Bruce Springsteen: Anyone who invites an audience member to share his stage and play music with him is okay by me.

7. Ian Chappell: Just there as a bullshit controller. To keep everybody on the straight and narrow.

8. Billy Joel: Acerbic, sardonic, smart, derisive, dismissive . . . the kind of bloke I like!

9. William McInnes: see below

10. Gadge: see above.

PB says LBJ would be interesting because, of all the people to be president, he was the one who seemed to enjoy it the most. I know what he means. There are recorded tapes of many presidential conversations. One of the most entertaining is LBJ phoning a startled tailor in Texas and promptly ordering several pairs of 'slacks'. Just the thing that the world's most powerful man should do with his time. He bangs on about how he has to have enough room in the crotch – 'that's my ball room', rasps away LBJ as he burps presidentially in between a list of demands.

Nixon plotted Watergate, Kennedy navigated the Cuban Missile Crisis and LBJ rambled on about his ball room.

'He was just buggerising about, but he was also a pendulum swinging from grand achievement to catastrophe. Very human, Falstaff, Richard the Third and Hamlet all wrapped into one ballroom!'

I say, 'Fair enough.'

And I look back at the list. I frown.

He bobbles his head.

'Christ! What now?'

I look up at him and back to the list.

'It's just a list,' he says. 'Doesn't mean anything.'

I look at him and ask why me and Gadge are there with these other blokes.

He asks me what I mean.

I say, 'Apart from the Natufian or Turk and the other fellow —'

'Egyptian,' PB details.

'Yes, the Egyptian, whoever it was who did the beer thing, these people are something.'

He says, 'So?'

I say, 'Me and Gadge?'

•

Gadge is another friend. An infuriating mixture of good humour, addiction to any newfangled gadget that may be the latest must-have (gadget – Gadge, nickname self-explanatory), an unending mind of useless trivia and a pal of rusted-on loyalty.

When we went off to Moreton Island for a weekend, we wafted along over the waters. The waters off the beach are dotted with wrecks, and there are other wrecks placed off the island which have become artificial reefs attracting all sorts of marine wildlife for snorkellers and divers to enjoy.

Gadge informed me there were even some old Brisbane trams which had been used as artificial reefs.

'Trams?' I asked.

Gadge nodded and said, 'Pretty certain there's some out there.' And he waved his hand to the water and said, 'Tickets, please.'

I always liked the old Brisbane trams. Some were set in municipal parks as playthings for kids. The trams soon ended up rusting away or were vandalised and I thought it was much better that they become a reef with passengers of fish, crabs, rays and the like.

I said this to Gadge. He nodded. 'That may be the case.'

Then he looked at me. 'Do you know that is the sort of shit talk that my father-in-law would come up with?'

I laughed.

'No, seriously, we were out here fishing once and it was a beautiful day. I told him about the trams, thought he might like to know – he's from Melbourne and they like their trams. He liked it, I think, but then he looked at me and said, "All those souls that those trams carried."'

Gadge shook his head. 'Like it was a faith lesson back at school – remember how they always used to say things like that? Some burley to set up a question and some poor prick would have to answer?'

I remembered. It was true. Some monotonous, droning, well-intentioned man of the cloth would stand in front of us, warbling, 'Look outside and see the beautiful playing oval we have here. Think of all the boys who have played out there as you have. Think of all of those boys.'

And there would be a pause as he walked slowly around the room and then came the slow intoning of the question. 'What do you think those boys would think when they were confronted by temptation? What would you do if you were tempted? Out there on the oval?'

Gadge laughed. 'I forgot the father-in-law used to be a teacher and a paid-up card-carrier in the old faith. And God help me, he answered that religious burley statement with the faith question.'

'He said, "Rodney,"' – that's Gadge's name – '"what would you think if you saw Jesus walking across these beautiful waters, above those old trams that carried all those souls?"'

Gadge laughed.

I asked him what he'd said in reply.

Gadge looked out at the water and said, 'I told him that I'd report a water hazard. Can't have some bloke wandering about through a boating channel. But if he was just looking at a tram then that was okay – he'd be the sort of bloke who could make public transport run on time. It'd take a fucking miracle.'

I laughed and Gadge shook his head. 'Still paying for that bit of low-rent smart-arseness.'

And then Gadge spent the next twenty minutes prattling about the performance rates of Metro buses and the Queensland Rail suburban system.

Gadge.

•

'So, why me and Gadge?' I ask PB. 'Why are we on the list?'

He says the list is of blokes he'd like to have a beer with and he just wanted to make sure there were a couple there he knew to be good blokes.

I think for a moment, and this makes me slightly uncomfortable. He is saying something nice . . . I think.

I tell him to fuck off.

He says, 'Up yours.'

We laugh.

'Gadge?' I say.

We laugh.

Then PB says, 'You don't have to make a list. There is no need for a reciprocal list.'

I have another sip and say that I don't think I would put PB on my list.

He looks at me and says, 'Fair enough.'

'But the bloke who made this Russian stout?' I tell him. 'He'd be on the list.'

PB nods his head. 'Good choice.'

I ask him if his Russian stout is the beer equivalent of two-minute noodles.

He just stares.

'You know, because you made them quickly.'

His head bobbles.

'You are a bloody idiot – that is something Gadge would say.'

Then we laugh together.

Sometimes it is odd the way men indicate that they are very fond of one another.

I ask PB if that was the point of the list.

He groans. 'What?'

'That you wanted to say Gadge and me were, you know . . .'

His head bobbles.

'You know, you like us, we're your –'

He cuts me off.

'I'm taking you off the bloody list!'

We laugh again.

And he says, 'It's just a silly list.'

•

Are lists always silly? Some can be. Especially ones centred on giving advice. Now there is a concept loaded with potential dread. Anytime anyone has come up to me and uttered quite pleasantly that they 'want a quiet word', I knew in my bones that I was about to be ripped a new arsehole.

Be it in a shouty land of aggro in a footy club or the more demure climate of a theatre, what started out as 'a quiet word' always ended up in an almighty bollocking. It's a euphemism cul-de-sac in which you're trapped, and you just have to breathe through it.

Even worse is when someone says, 'Just a word to the wise' – which means you are going to be bored senseless by advice given solely through the prism of that person's blinkered view of life. Or the offerings of people who behave like Agony Aunts and Agony Uncles who, for some reason, believe they possess the skills to steer other people through life.

They call their tips 'Life Hacks', which is code for getting around life like a hacker gets around a computer's defences: supplanting the programs and resetting the software.

This sort of advice is usually cut and pasted from someplace on the web and is assured of being foolproof. It's mostly old hat and hand-me-down in tone and substance.

We have another Russian stout.

'I'll give you the good oil' is always muttered in the guise of a friendly threat. Basically it's a situation where it's 'my way or the highway'. The information being imparted is from a well-informed source, meaning that it can only be ignored at your own risk.

PB and I talk about being a good bloke. We make another list. Why? Because we want to offer an alternative word to the wise, a bit of a tip, some good oil. It can be a risk offering advice, but we think it's worth a crack because there's a multitude of books, blogs, websites etc. available, all providing information, advice, and guidance on how to live your life, how to live someone else's life or how to have a positive and lasting impact on someone else. Midlife crisis? A million sites. How to raise children? Blogs, websites abound. Difficult teenager? Books, books, books. But strangely, as far as our limited ability to surf a web has found, there's a dearth of information afforded to what we consider one of the most vulnerable, unsure, and susceptible demographics in society – the young man in his early twenties. Having endured the triumphs, tribulations, and awkwardness of his teenage years, having left home, having his first serious job, relationship, crisis, confrontation with mortality, he is perhaps a little wanting in advice.

So, over a few more jars of home brew, PB and I decided to offer sage-like, honest, and heartfelt advice to our sons, both of whom are in their early to mid twenties. These aren't life hacks or agony aunts or handyman hints, or 'words to the wise'. Just a few tips from two boofheads who have been there, been around the block a few times and have hopefully learnt a few things along the way.

1. Never touch a woman in anger. Never.
2. Before you go out on a date, do two things at least: shower, and decide which is more important – your phone or your date. Only take one with you.

3. A beer glass is designed for one thing only and ever – to hold beer.
4. Your friends might need you to listen to them occasionally – let yourself be the listener.
5. See all, ignore much, do a little – in all situations. Most battles are Pyrrhic.
6. Bouncers will generally want to have the last word – let them.
7. Winning isn't everything. Full stop. The only person you ever, ever, need to best is the person you were yesterday. To validate yourself by comparison is ultimately self-defeating, self-delusional and eventually painful and unrewarding.
8. You are not indispensable, but you are irreplaceable.
9. Your values as a human are revealed by what you do when no one is watching.
10. Most problems aren't.
11. If money solves it, it was never a problem in the first place.
12. Engage in (slightly) risky behaviour but do so sober and sequentially and incrementally.
13. We have the greatest beaches in the world – use them.
14. Travel.
15. Eat heartily. There will be a time when the weight is easy to gain and hard to lose, but it is not when you are in your early twenties!
16. Learn to make a good cheese sauce. It covers most culinary misadventures and inadequacies.

17. Look outside the circuitry of yourself – do something for others regularly, anonymously, passionately, voluntarily.
18. It is true that nothing good happens after midnight in a pub, bar or nightclub.
19. Save 10 per cent of your salary/wage, every week. That way, you'll get rich slowly, but you will get rich.
20. The music your parents listen to is actually quite good.
21. Ask your fathers, uncles, elders, whatever you'd call them, for a list of men they think they'd like to have a beer with. And get them to explain why.
22. Always act with kindness.

Just the thoughts of two middle-aged boofheads and I know the life that confronts our daughters and our children, however they define themselves, will have other adventures and travails but I think there's a few keepers there for the lads.

CHAPTER 10

BUSINESS TIME

I went to get some new specs not so long ago after there'd been a few incidents with my perfectly fine prescription glasses. Two pairs.

I had sensibly sat on one pair when I was travelling in an airliner. I had been trying to find them in a bag up in the overhead locker and was asked by a steward to return to my seat as the plane had begun its descent. I nodded and apologised, saying I'd been trying to find my specs.

When I sat, I swore. The air steward looked back at me. I held up a hand and said, 'I think I just found my glasses.'

They were, of course, in my back pocket.

The other pair I had at first tried to protect by buying a collection of wretched magnifying off-the-shelf specs from a chemist down the road. Why? It seemed like a good idea at the time. These glasses had the effect of making me look like a rather baroque character from a Federico Fellini film.

The plus side was that I could lose or break or throw them with relative impunity. This last – throwing – I admit, is perhaps a slight flaw in my character. I've had the occasional tendency to throw whatever might be in my hand at a given moment when I crack the sads. Not always, but just enough for it to be commented on by those who know me. Especially my aunt, who used to take great delight when I was teased by one of my sisters and was too small to do anything about it other than scream and throw my half-eaten Weiss ice-cream bar to the ground in anger and then howl in despair when I realised what I had done.

It was a party trick that also brought great delight to others in my family.

I was a chucker. And my aunt used to laugh and say with gusto, 'Here's Meckiff to bowl!'

This was in reference to Ian Meckiff, an early 1960s Australian Test cricketer whose career was cut short by accusations of 'chucking': throwing when he bowled. It eventually forced him out of the game, with a little help from complaining English journalists and a compliant Donald Bradman.

My father would call me the Man from Munster, a reference apparently based around a friend of his who had once played Hurling, a strange game beloved by the Irish, for Munster. It took me years to understand this. Though Hurling is what I tended to do with objects when a sook set in.

At first, I thought he was referring to Herman Munster, a TV show character who was a half–Frankenstein's monster half-clown who would howl and do a funny dance when he was 'emotional'.

Oddly enough, years later a potential romance was nipped in the bud on a trip to the beach when the young woman witnessed me surfing. I thought I had displayed a Kelly Slater–like ability on my brother's old Malibu board by standing upright occasionally. I stood stock-still with arms outstretched in the manner of the Christ the Redeemer statue on the peak overlooking Rio de Janeiro. Then, pleased with myself, I would wobble and lift my feet and fall into the waves with a howl.

She told me that she liked me, but that I looked like Herman Munster.

Our romance ended and she began another with a mate who could surf in an un-Herman Munsterlike fashion.

So, back to my specs. Absent-mindedness had set in when I was watching the cricket. I should have known that I was using the good glasses that I was saving because the bloody things let me see, unlike the chemist magnifiers, which made everything look like some bad *Countdown* music video from the '80s.

I put the forgetfulness down to frustration.

I was frustrated because Pat Cummins paid no attention to my repeated advice to him. I was trying to advise Pat not to bowl short to Pommy tail-enders. 'Stop bowling short Pat to these bloody flogs!' Pat bowled short, got top-edged for six and some gangling, supercilious Pommy with an overbite smiled giddily.

I stood, yelled, and threw my glasses against a wall and then screamed in realisation of what I had done. I made a mental note to book an appointment at the optometrist, and wished that Pat would do to the wickets what I'd done to my specs – shatter them.

I also burst out laughing. I had seen my reflection in the panes of the French doors and had to admit it was quite amusing. Perhaps my family had a point in making fun of me.

'Meckiff to bowl!' I cried, and did a Herman Munster dance.

I thought of my aunt and my dad.

And my old flame. I hoped she had gone on and had a cracking time.

I felt unaccountably happy thinking of them all.

•

Inevitably, I found myself at the optometrist, where a young man enquired why I needed new glasses. I mumbled something about losing my old pair and yawned.

I apologised, and said that I had been up late watching the cricket.

The young man said he had been up late last night as well.

'Were you watching the cricket?' Perhaps he had shared some advice with Pat.

'No,' he said. 'I was up late with my Young Adult Group Night at my church.'

I took that in and thought to myself that whatever a church Young Adult Group Night entailed (it did sound like a charge sheet because of the way he pronounced it – 'Young Adult Grope Night'), it wouldn't have been anything like me and my late night, a late-middle-aged man screaming in a slightly unhinged manner at a wonderful cricketer on the other side of the world via my ridiculously large television screen.

So I said, 'Good for you.'

He said, 'Indeedy. Now, have you been arrived?'

I thought he'd said something he didn't mean – or I had misheard?

'Sorry?' I said.

'Arrived. Have you been arrived?'

I still didn't understand.

'Have your details been entered? Have you been arrived?'

He said this in a manner which indicated that he could not quite understand why I had no comprehension of the way the word 'arrived' was being used.

'I've never heard that word been used that way before,' I told him.

He smiled a little and said, 'Yeah, I guess so, but that's the language of the business.'

What a thing to hear and witness. Business evolving language – of course, people like to conjugate a verb but torturing the essence of a word to give it a superficial meaning of efficient practice is a worthless thing to pursue. I asked if the young man from the church Young Adult Grope Night had a learnings processing compartment in relation to my having been arrived.

He looked up and said, yes, as a matter of fact he did have a Learnings section. 'For self-assessment, we mark down the messages we want to take from the Learnings of each transaction and pool them in a weekly meeting.'

I suddenly felt very normal yelling at the telly and breaking my glasses.

Learnings and arrived and misspoke, running an idea up a flagpole, lots of moving parts, let's unpack this, progress this, move forward, take stock, make a specific emotional inventory, spreadsheet a concept, rationalise a presentation and a hundred other pieces of drivel that the evolution of 'the language of business' has given us. It wasn't just this optometrist — they were nice people who sold good glasses — it was the whole concept of business-speak.

It's like a secret code of drivel that supposedly means efficiency and best practice. I thought to myself that I longed for the old-school, 'How can we help?' or 'What can I do for you?'

Basic and to the point.

And then I thought, no, that is cherry-picking the past.

Every part of life, whatever the endeavour, has its own lingo, business talk is just a heightened example of the transactional nature of life. It's smart business to jazz up communications, to make it seem like what is happening is something special and unique.

A paradigm shift, for example, is prime business-speak, yet that was coined in 1962. Rightsizing is from the 1980s and basically means sacking people and eliminating services to optimise profits.

But things change, and whether they change for the best depends on the perspective of whoever is speaking, a case of 'taking in the view from our present summit'. That metaphor was from a financial planner who 'was 'sherpa-ing' a friend through a home loan 'trek' until they could plant the flag when they had reached 'ultimate summit'.

The financial planner proudly told my friend that he had come up with these terms himself.

This example, I think it safe to say, is just guff.

It's interesting, though, that in the process of selling stuff to people sometimes words and expressions become adopted by people outside the direct intention of flogging a product.

Advertising. It should be business talk. But it can go in directions that no one anticipates.

In 1954 a jingle was created for the breakfast spread of breakfast spreads, Vegemite. A yeast-based spread that has been the staple of lunch boxes and breakfasts for decades, it was considered a health food, a beneficial product in growing healthy children for a healthy vibrant nation and the 1954 jingle was a perfect example of that boundless optimism of the post–World War II nation-building era.

It was almost as if Vegemite was the definitive code for what Australia was. Children in military-type dress-ups, dancing girls and boys in tiny solider uniforms, marching and dancing in step, doing their duty growing up being healthy Australians. Happy children sing a happy song about a happy breakfast spread, Happy Little Vegemites. Mummy said that we are growing stronger every week, growing strong as Australians, growing strong as a nation. 'Mummy' could almost take on the meaning of motherland.

And I am perfectly fine with that. I love Vegemite. That smell of so many breakfasts, a happy start to the day. Opening up a plastic lunch box at school and breathing in a Vegemite sanger on white buttered bread was enough to signal that whatever had happened during school lessons, I was now in the oasis of big lunch, free from regimentation and the expectation of knowledge and learning being forced down my throat.

Heavens, as I grew older, I even put Vegemite in spag bol. Or spaghetti bolognaise to those not *au fait* with the kitchen lingo of Australia.

So iconic was this campaign that the phrase seeped into the national psyche and 'Happy Little Vegemites' came to mean a group of people who were content, on message and happy with their lot in life.

Sometimes, though, the vernacular can take atmospheric intention to a whole new level of nightmarish compliance.

About thirty-two years after the first time the Happy Little Vegemites ad aired, I found myself, along with a collection of other middle-class suburban Australians, at drama school. At WAAPA – which, although it sounds like a fast-food product, is the highly regarded West Australian Academy of Performing Arts.

Drama school was always going to be a bit of a trip in many ways because even though there's a multitude of disciplines to get your head around, the whole concept of 'acting' is also a rather nebulous one. Plus, the mid to late '80s was a time of New Age and Alternative ideas of movement, meditation and learning so there were crackpots, nutjobs and would-be gurus plying their trade alongside practical and professional educators.

So, for every crackpot who insisted that tai chi-ing in a park across the road was the best way to understand the essence of movement instead of in a purpose-built studio – conveniently forgetting that the park was full of bindis, which resulted in something like a rather frenetic Martha Graham interpretive dance piece with people springing about yelping – there would also be dedicated teachers who'd guide you through the theories of performance.

There was a fair bit of wank involved but students had also bought in and were committed, so the best thing was to have the safety valve of being able to take the piss when needed.

It still didn't stop you from existing in a rather rarefied atmosphere, which could lead to having one's head firmly up one's arse.

And so it came to pass that we attended a drama festival held in a lovely rural area, somewhere in the sticks east of Perth. The festival happened to be a week after many students had been told by one of the dance teachers to go to a screening of a French film entitled *The Young Girls of Rochefort*. It was very French. Lots of bright colours, amazingly attractive people, Gene Kelly in a toupee that looked like it had come from a show bag or pinched from a low-rent Elvis impersonator – and dancing. Lots of dancing.

Funny, bendy, dainty dancing, almost self-consciously precious. As if the Tony Bartuccio Dancers from the *Don Lane Show* were all on speed.

With these images fresh in our minds, we descended upon the country town. One of our number swept through an op shop and stepped forth onto the street in an outfit that wouldn't have been out of place in any scene of *The Young Girls of Rochefort*. White pants, pastel shirt, green in colour, complete with pastel tie, purple in colour. 'Hey!' he proclaimed in a well-vowelled actor-in-training voice, 'I'm dancing like a Frenchman!' And he attempted to dance a la *The Young Girls of Rochefort*, slightly inhibited by the fact that he was wearing Dr Scholl health sandals and he couldn't dance a lick in the first place. 'Pizza Feet' was a nickname given to him by a dance teacher, who described him as being unique in his teaching career. 'I have never seen flatter feet and any one person so devoid of coordinated or rhythmic movement.'

'Thank you,' replied Pizza Feet. 'It's a talent I was born with.'

'Indeed, Pizza Feet, indeed,' replied the teacher.

As we journeyed through the evening, an increasingly recreationally enhanced Pizza Feet continued to dance like a Frenchman in a more and more animated and enthusiastically uncoordinated manner. Somewhere along the way, one of us acquired a garden gnome from the verandah of a pub we entered, because he thought the gnome looked like Bob Hawke. He promptly stuck Bob Gnome Hawk down the front of his rather ostentatious 'actor's' coat, just to keep old Bob warm.

We ended up camping in said pub where people in lumber jackets and with hard workers' faces were also spending their Saturday night. We stood out like sore thumbs.

Pizza Feet, the dancing Frenchman, wobbled around the pub with a meat tray that he had won, waltzing with his bangers, steaks, rissoles and chops, doing his meat tray *Swan Lake*. I was trying to interest a couple of locals in the benefits of the Alexander technique when all at once everything went truly pear-shaped. A local had recognised the gnome down the front of the ostentatious actor's ostentatious actor's coat.

'You've pinched my bloody Bob Hawke, you bastard. Hey Pat, they nicked our Bob Hawke gnome!'

Whoever Pat was wasn't clear as our chum apologetically pointed to the gnome down his coat.

'Well, I told you he looked like Bob Hawke!' said our ostentatious acting chum. 'I was keeping him warm while we wait for a drink.'

And our ostentatious actor tried to remove Bob Hawke from his coat but in doing so managed only to push him down, then further down, until the gnome slid down slowly, gripped by our chum's legs until he could hold the Bob Gnome no more and the thing plopped onto the ground with a wobble.

'Ah, *mon Dieu!*' said Pizza Feet the dancing Frenchman in a bad French accent, 'You 'ave given birth to ze gnome!'

'I'm going to name him Bob,' said our ostentatious overcoated friend.

This was when we heard Pat.

'Pick up the gnome and put it on the bar.'

We all turned to a doorway which was filled and then dwarfed by one of the largest human beings I have ever seen. He was a walking eclipse. A truly huge man. I could see that he was a walloper, a police officer, for he had his uniform on beneath a throwover jacket. Off duty.

We all looked at him and he raised a mighty hand and pointed to the gnome.

'Put the gnome on the bar.'

He stressed almost every syllable in a deep, almost deadpan, manner. He sounded like John Wayne's Australian cousin.

Overcoat picked up the gnome and put him on the bar. Pat moved towards us.

'Boys in town for the drama do.'

We nodded.

'Having a bit of fun?' he said.

Pizza Feet said slowly, 'I won ze meat tray.'

Pat nodded gravely. 'Yes, I can see that. You want to be careful you don't lose your load, some of those snags look they could go any second.'

Pizza Feet nodded and put the meat tray on the table. He thought for a moment.

'I'll think I'll donate ze meat tray back to ze footy club.'

'Good of you. And you'll put Bob back on the verandah. And I'll buy you a beer. And then you can get on with your night a bit more quietly.'

And Pat paused, looking immense, and said – without any menace, but somehow making the words seem like the most chilling any of us had ever heard – 'Now, are you Happy Little Vegemites? Or do I have to put a rose in every cheek?'

Making a wholesome marketing tagline for a breakfast spread sound truly terrifying was a gift that Pat the Eclipse truly had, and I thought it was perhaps not the first time he had uttered those words.

We were all Happy Little Vegemites and quietened down. The footy club shouted us another round for Pizza Feet's generosity in handing back the meat tray and a good-natured haggling took place over Overcoat's purchasing of the Bob Hawke gnome.

But to this day, when I enjoy a Vegemite sanger or on toast or in spag bol, I hear those words and the hairs on the back of my neck rise.

•

When a phrase takes hold and is adopted by the people it can outlive the product that the words were designed to sell.

In the late '90s the Yellow Pages business directory was a large paperback book listing thousands of companies' business details that could help customers choose where and on what they would like to spend their hard-earned.

These huge books used to just appear on the verandah or at the front door yearly and seemed as constant as the sun.

The internet changed all that. Suddenly one year they simply stopped appearing, but their memory lingers on.

A television advertisement of a boss trying to find the company's listing in the Yellow Pages begins with a polite question the boss knows the answer to. 'Jan? Where's our ad in the Yellow Pages directory? Jan?'

There's a close-up of a worker hearing the question, a deadpan look and then turning and running out of the office. The boss tries to keep calm, counting to ten slowly and then as she sees Jan running down the street can contain herself no longer, and screams, 'Not happy, Jan!' out the window.

It is funny and well performed and well made. But somehow that phrase 'Not happy, Jan!' has managed to stay about in the cultural landscape of Australia.

On a television set where whatever we were trying to shoot was taking forever, I overheard two grips speaking. They were sure that the first assistant director was going to call for overtime. It is never welcomed but on a Friday evening it was going to be even less popular, with everyone wanting to start their weekend.

'Looks like he's going to call for OT,' said the older grip.

'Overtime? You reckon?' said the younger grip.

'I do,' said the older grip.

The younger grip took this in and then breathed out slowly.

'Not happy, Jan.'

The older grip looked surprised and then laughed. 'What did you say?'

'Not happy, Jan,' repeated the younger grip.

'You know where that comes from? That saying? You heard of the Yellow Pages?'

'Nuh' said the younger grip. 'But I know it means I'm not happy.'

The older grip smiled and said, 'Fair enough.' He saw me looking at him and then added with a smile. 'We're getting old, Willy. We can remember the Yellow Pages. Good old Jan!'

Indeed.

Lord knows how people's minds work and what they dredge up from their memory at certain times in their lives. At a barbecue I was helping myself to a beer after exchanging hellos with one of our hosts, who was burning sausages and hamburgers and aptly dressed in an apron emblazoned with the words, 'Chief Tucker Fucker Upper-er', when a group of women I knew were laughing uproariously and one of them called out to me. 'He grew up in Queensland, let's ask William.'

The only man amongst them was this woman's partner and he tried his best to give me fair warning. 'Oh, leave him out of it.'

'You just be quiet, my love,' the woman said to her partner with warmth but also with a hint of mischief.

I thought this might be a bit problematic but also a bit of fun, so I went over and asked, 'What's up?'

The man rolled his eyes.

One of the women said, 'We were just talking about the stupid things that men have said to us after having sex and we thought you could help.'

'Oh, turn it up,' was all that I could manage.

'Come on,' they all chorused. 'We just need help with a bit of context.'

'Oh, turn it up,' was all that I could manage again. I was asked if I had ever said anything stupid.

'Oh probably,' I mumbled.

The man sorrowfully shook his head.

'Oh, turn it up,' said a woman. They laughed, as I did.

I thought for a bit and then offered this chestnut.

'I did tell somebody, after we'd been on the job, that I had missed my bus.'

'You romantic!' was the reply.

I shrugged my shoulders. 'It was a spontaneous bit of exercise that hijacked the morning. I wasn't complaining but I was late for where I had to be.'

'Oh, you really are a romantic.'

I was told I was full of euphemisms.

And I was also told that it wasn't the dumbest thing that had been uttered. One of my chums said that a man told her that she should have lots of daughters.

'He didn't?' I asked.

She nodded. 'Meaning I should have daughters so other blokes could have a nice time.'

'Well at least he was appreciative,' somebody said.

'Yeah, and also a bit creepy.'

This was agreed.

'What sort of context can I give?' I asked.

'You grew up in Queensland, didn't you? Around the same time as me?' an old friend asked.

I assured her that I had.

'You remember the Man from Nescafé ad?'

I thought for a bit and said, 'The one shot in the Glass House Mountains?'

My friend laughed, clapped her hands, and said, 'Yes! That's the one.'

Her husband rolled his eyes.

I was asked to describe the ad. It was from the late '70s and was supposedly set in some South American–type country, which was a joke because the helicopter that flew in at the beginning of the ad, backlit by the sun, chugged past the backdrop of the Glass House Mountains.

The Glass House Mountains, undoubtedly spectacular, are about as Queensland as you can get: a set of volcanic plugs printed on a million tea towels.

The helicopter landed and a man in a safari suit, aviator sunglasses and a big bushy porn-star moustache climbed down and presented himself to a group of 'villagers'. These were extras made up to look like somebody in an advertising agency's imagination of coffee-growing South Americans. Which meant badly made-up people wearing white shift cotton clothing, sombreros and colourful ponchos thrown over a shoulder or two.

The man with the porn-star moustache slowly approached the anxious Southeast Queensland/South American coffee-growers.

A young woman offered him a cup, he took it, smelt it, then took a sip.

Anxious eyes watched him, the villagers held their breaths, the man took another sip, lifted his head and nodded as a breathless voice-over boomed, 'The Man from Nescafé says ... YES!'

The villagers throw their sombreros, dancing breaks out, they cheer, the young woman smiles, music swells, it's an almost orgasmic display of Southeast Queensland/South American civic pride. And the Man from Nescafé gets back into his helicopter, which climbs into the skies.

'My god, William, you do remember the ad,' said my pal. She looked to her partner and back at me. 'Was this a Queensland boy thing?'

'Turn it up,' I said, to a few groans. 'It's just a silly old ad.'

'Oh really?' she said. 'This ad is how old?'

'Oh lord, decades old. Decades. Maybe forty years,' I said.

'Forty years. Well, not too long ago I was having a lovely time with someone I care a lot about and there we were in post-coital afterglow.'

'Oh, come on, turn it up,' said the woman's partner and there was laughter. It was also obvious who she was talking about.

'And we held each other, and we looked into each other's eyes, and he seemed like he was going to say something that meant a great deal to him. He looked down and he said slowly . . .' She paused, and I admit even I wanted to know what the words were.

She took a breath. And then paused again, before carrying on. 'He looked at me and said, "The Man from Nescafé says YES!"'

There was silence for a moment. Then I erupted in laughter.

'What were you thinking?' I almost shrieked.

'Exactly!' said his partner.

The man fluttered his hands a little and said, 'We can't all have buses we miss, William. I have no idea what I was thinking about, but at least it was better than saying "Forty-three beans in every cup".'

More laughter. The woman reached out and held her partner's hand and through laughter said, 'You lovely old plonker.'

I sat in the optometrist and burst out laughing. The young man looked at me and asked me, 'Everything all right?'

Why wouldn't everything be all right? We have such a wonderful way with words and though the language of business might grate, what we pull from the past and create is delightful.

I nodded and replied, 'The man from Nescafé says yes!' And laughed again.

CHAPTER 11

CALLING TIME

It had been a run-of-the-mill end of the weekend. A Sunday arvo sinking in predictable fashion with everybody mooching about, half turning their minds to the week ahead and then thinking, why bother, why not just go down with the sun? Monday could take care of itself, and the rest of the week would follow. I would have been in my mid-teens. Peak gormless period for me. It had been the year of my perm, where I had been packed off to a barber for a shear but instead of a short back and sides had come back with a hairstyle resembling a clown from some circus.

I walked in and my mother had turned to say hello, seen me and then screamed, 'Jesus Christ!' My father ran in, interrupted from a little weekend work on some banana trees with his machete, and asked protectively, 'What is it, 'Ris?' Then he saw me and screamed. Pointed the machete at me and said, 'Christ alive, boy, when I was your age, I was jumping out of planes fighting Germans — for what!' And he pointed the machete at me again to accentuate the point.

The perm was gone by the end of the next weekend, but it had made a lasting impression.

'Cop an eyeful of this,' would welcome my appearance whenever I came into my parents' presence. 'At least he's got a sensible pill chop.'

They laughed about it almost as soon as they had yelled. They never really harboured a grudge for very long and I remember that not long after the machete had been pointed at me, my father said quite warmly, 'Oh well, this one is probably the idiot. You'd better learn to juggle if you want to keep that 'do. Might earn a quid.'

But on that end of the weekend, there was a lazy accepting feel to the house and backyard. My father had prowled around a bit and made a bit of a half-hearted effort in being cantankerous, asking occasionally, 'You right?' to me, but soon he was asking even the dog and giving him an accompanying pat and scratch. Then soon enough he and my mother stood together watering some plants and looking at their favourite part of the day.

'Cop an eyeful of that,' one of them would say of the sky above.

'Come here, Cabbagehead,' my father would say to me. 'Come and fill your boots with this.' And he'd flick his head to the sky.

'You should,' my mother would say, 'try to remember a view like this,' and she'd have a bit of a ruminate.

'Keeps you honest.'

I remembered my father showing me the Christmas beetle. Good things happened in that backyard, but as a teenager I sort of thought the view thing was only for my parents.

Sometimes it just takes a while. I woke up the other morning and, after having eased into the day with a cuppa, I thought to myself, not for the first time, I owe a debt of gratitude to Alexandra Widt for making me understand the glory of the inward eye. I've written before about sitting in a dreadful literature elective tutorial at uni with people banging on about their favourite verse or two. Alexandra Widt came up with, 'I Wandered Lonely as A Cloud' by William Wordsworth.

Most will know the poem. A fellow walking along sees a vast number of yellow flowers waving in the wind, thinks it's lovely and remembers it. That's it.

Monty Python used to do a skit with a Gumby Yorkshireman complete with knotted hanky on head reciting the poem like a loon.

That's where I first came across it.

But Alexandra Widt started talking about this poem that made her feel like crying.

Honesty isn't something you come across much when you are nineteen, especially in a literature tutorial. Everyone is so busy trying to stay awake or trying to think of what they can say that will get a good mark.

Alexandra Widt explained how this poem made her feel.

How the fellow who saw the flowers knew they were lovely but didn't really appreciate the beauty until later.

Later, when he was alone, when he remembered that beauty, it was so bittersweet, and expressed in some of the loveliest lines found in a poem:

> For oft, when on my couch I lie
> In vacant or in pensive mood,
> They flash upon that inward eye
> Which is the bliss of solitude;

'It's so sad, that he saw the beauty but didn't understand just what it meant to him. Somehow, he's lost something, but in that one moment, however brief, he holds it in his imagination.'

I remember her pausing and saying, 'It just seems so human, to pass on something and then later, after it's gone, you realise what you've held, somewhere inside you. And perhaps you still hold it. It makes me want to cry, from happiness or sadness I don't know.'

Let me tell you, I thought her words were impressive back when I was a ragged-headed droob at nineteen and now, as a middle-aged boofhead, I think them even more so.

It's a gift to be reminded of the magic of the inward eye.

That morning I'd woken up and thought of the view you have when you walk along Redcliffe's shoreline from the Redcliffe jetty towards Scarborough, and what the view gives you. No matter how much development has occurred, and there's been plenty, for that is the way of things, that perspective out across the bay has remained almost unchanged for ages.

I can easily imagine my parents looking at the view before I was born, daytrippers from the steamers from Brisbane to the peninsula in the 1920s, perhaps convicts from the first settlement, and Indigenous Australians who made their home there long before colonisation.

I felt inexplicably calmed and warmed by that view in my inward eye, as if in a way I connected to all who'd seen it.

There is something wonderful and utterly human about being comforted by a memory of a view in your mind's eye, as if isolation is defeated or at least put at bay by a simple act of being human.

And the same with a view from the back deck of a City Cat on the way to St Lucia, where I saw a Brisbane sunset split the open sky with an explosion of red–orange glory. Looking up at a high rise along the river, I saw someone silhouetted standing on a balcony, their arms outstretched as if they were trying to touch the gorgeous colours of the sky.

I thought the views lovely when I saw them with my eyes, but oddly they became more beautiful when I remembered them with that inward eye. Maybe we just take things for granted and don't appreciate what we see. Perhaps that's what it means to ruminate: you think about what you may see. And when you see it, and think about it, you might understand it a bit more. I don't mean you have disappeared up you own arse, though that is always a risk with any human endeavour, but it's worth having a go. A case of getting our hands off it and having a good hard look at ourselves, as Billy Walsh, the captain of the Emerald Hill Cricket Club's fourth grade team, advised us all when faced with the problem of the team playing with even remote competence.

•

I've always found it slightly odd that our national day is held on the day of the arrival of the First Fleet in 1788. It's an important date to remember, but is it our national day? Yet that long weekend in January can make you ruminate. When you have a gander around, the things you see when you cop an eyeful.

The 26th of January. I grew up with that date being Australia Day. It never seemed like it was much of a deal. Maybe a parade or a community concert with little giveaways and a sausage sizzle. It mattered when something like the Australia Day Floods in 1974 happened. But then it only mattered to people in Brisbane, where the floods took place. Australia Day was Australia Day, like it always was. Although, in truth, it had always been a bit malleable. It was first proclaimed

Australia Day in 1935 and it wasn't until 1994 that it became a public holiday consistently across Australia. I remember people getting upset that the holiday would be celebrated on the 26th even if it fell on a weekday and would not be tacked onto a weekend. Ripped off! I heard a colleague from a television show cry when it was announced. The best people got was adding a Monday if the date fell on a Saturday or Sunday.

Later, it started to become a point of reference in the cultural debate around Australia's identity. I must admit that if I thought about it, I thought it odd that we didn't have a national day that celebrated when we became a federated nation. The day we became master, as much as we can be, of our own destiny. The day we ran the show, responsible for what we did and for what happened in our nation.

America has the 4th of July as Independence Day, France has Bastille Day, India has the 26th of January as Republic Day, and the list goes on. Days when a nation threw off the yoke of empire or monarchy through revolution or democratic progression.

We celebrate our national day when Arthur Phillip arrived with the First Fleet, a bunch of convicts mostly, and planted a British flag on a land they probably didn't even want to be any part of. And didn't really care or know about what had gone on before. Arthur Phillip had a crack at trying to come to some kind of terms with the original Australians, but it didn't seem to go that well. It was as if Australia only started in 1788, which is a bit rich, really, all that history of what had gone on before never thought important enough to understand or embrace.

And yet I can't be blind to the fact that if the flag-planting hadn't taken place, somebody like me wouldn't have enjoyed the life I have in this country. I like being who I am and where I come from.

Also, the fact that our Federation Day is the first of January is a problem, celebration-wise. I can imagine the communal cry of 'Ripped off!' if our national day were to become a day that is already a public holiday. Although, perhaps if one of the public holidays was moved to the second as compensation, that might find a few supporters. 'You beauty! We've doubled up.'

Maybe the date we choose can have a more generous feel, a more inclusive embracing of the past.

•

Australia Day is the last gasp of the summer holidays, the bright light burning brightly before the filament breaks and we are all plunged into the year proper. School begins, business stirs and tries to get itself moving, and the great Australian collective being heaves itself into the year.

So, it seemed appropriate, on this national long weekend, to apprise oneself of the places which typify where we live. The Australian beach is simply the greatest stage play of Australia. So much colour, so much movement. So much choreography, so many players, bit parts, hams, walk-ins, extras. So many costumes, so quick-moving that the audience is never bored.

And unlike most pursuits, any body shape, size, ability and level of expertise is accounted for on the beach. So many different members to the multicultural cast of the Australian Beach.

Going to the beach is the most egalitarian activity that I know of, apart from sleeping.

There are, of course, some players as chiselled as if they have stepped out of a Marvel superhero movie. Encased in budgie-smugglers, a buffed-beyond-belief suburban Thor half struts, half strolls slowly into the water as if he could almost part the waves, towering above an old nonna admonishing a wayward grandchild for throwing wet sand pies at his sibling.

As a wave breaks over suburban Thor's vitals, he lets out the universal intake of breath before shrieking and waving his hands. The nonna turns, sees him, laughs and mimics him.

Suburban Thor and Nonna laugh together.

Seeing so many people engage in such welcoming activity is to see the basic glory of the human body. From the truly beautiful butterfly-like movements of young children to the staggeringly graceful paddle boarder, slicing through the deeper water with her stand-up paddle.

And there are some guests on the Australian beach stage, some backpackers from England, bouncing a soccer ball from head to head. Perhaps it's uncharitable, but when I watched them arrive earlier, I thought, They are for roasting. Now, near lunch and about to head off, I think their skin should be used as a colour guide for Bunnings Paints – from '8 am English' to 'Midday Pink'.

Kids are everywhere, as are their smiles and giggles. Whether it is the sheer joy of feeling a quick wave splash over them, or through them, knowing they are safe in mum or dad's arms, or catching their first wave on a boogie board, their noise is so comforting. The smell of the sea and that particular atmosphere of the beach. Children and seagulls shrieking, the sound of waves, the sand under your feet and rising between your toes, your feet squeaking in the sand while you run.

It's the families. All the slip, slop, slapping, the grimacing faces as sunscreen is applied. The excitement and wonder that children have for the beach. I sit and watch and remember how my children giggled and splashed with me, stared at the rock pools and jumped from my shoulders into the waves. Just as I did with my father.

I see a parent holding her toddler's hand, and I think of how they, as Indigenous Australians, are the most ancient continuous civilisation on earth and as contemporary as everyone else on the beach. I feel my children's hand in mine and mine in my father's.

Life on the beach goes on and we with it.

A village of sandcastles with the mandatory moat is crumbled as the tide flows in. One of the sweetest and most melancholic passages of time.

Amid the chaos of the cast, I notice another ceremony and ritual beginning. Between the beach cricket, wayward frisbees and tossed footballs, a small gathering of men under a gazebo go quiet. Together, they turn to one direction and commence their prayer. It is the appropriate time of the day.

Once completed, they fire up the barbie, while down the way a dog shakes himself dry over his howling owners, a band of teenagers gorge on Maccas and a couple in retro togs from some old '80s Alpine ciggy advertisement eat celery sticks and take selfies.

What a stage play. What a cast of characters. And even better, though the long weekend may finish, the season of the beach and the best of Australia doesn't have a limited run.

Unlike us. You and me.

All things must pass. George Harrison had a successful album by that name in his first post-Beatles outing and he conveniently pinched the title from the Gospel of Matthew in the Bible. If you've been around long enough you'll understand whatever spiritual meanings George and Matthew the ex-taxman had, there's a pure cut and dried meaning to that elegant phrase, 'All things must pass' – everything has a use-by date.

All of us drop off the perch. Or cark it. Or pull up stumps. Or buy it. Or croak it. Or, in basic biological parlance, we die. Whatever our faith system might be, we cease to exist. It's not something we like to think about, but it happens.

During a Covid lockdown I got news about a life having ended. Colin Forsythe had died.

He was a unit manager on film and television productions. One of those names that whizz past in a blur as the credits roll at the end of a show.

He worked on every episode of *Blue Heelers*, a show about country policing that first appeared in 1994, eventually running for thirteen seasons.

It was a funny old thing, at times a bit clunky, but people liked it enough to remember it fondly.

I was in the show for four seasons, leaving in 1998. Decades ago.

When I went for a drive-through Covid test (for a while a drive-through was no longer a fast-food hit but meant having a swab in your mouth and one up a nostril), I was asked by the very capable medical professional conducting the sweeping, 'Excuse me, but weren't you in *Blue Heelers*?'

As my nostrils were the only part of my body on display when the question was asked, the young medical professional must've been a very keen viewer of the show indeed.

I asked how she could tell as it was over twenty years ago since I had appeared, and she'd be lucky if she was twenty-two herself.

She said she was twenty-three and had watched it on a streaming service and promptly waved me on.

So, *Blue Heelers* is still popular. Actors always get remembered, the faces on the telly in the corner, on digital devices you carry anywhere.

People wouldn't know about a bloke like Colin Forsythe.

Unit managers are the first to turn up and the last to go. They feed, tend and provide basic infrastructure for the shoot to go ahead.

And if they're like Col, they care, commiserate, share and become a friend.

A car fixed, errand run, a favour given free, party pies, something nice to drink on wrap and his words of goodbye, 'Hooroo. Travel well.'

Hooroo. People think the old Australian word for farewell is a made-up affectation. Maybe it can be and maybe people might think Col was a cliché.

Col was as rough as guts and epically incorrect on occasions, but he had a heart as big as the outback and was a generous soul. I never heard Col say a bad word about anybody. Colourful words maybe, and some I'd never heard before, but never bad or malicious.

I once bumped into him at our local library, and he boomed out hello and said he was there with his mate Blythe, whom Col always called 'Blyffe'.

'Oh yeah,' I said.

'Yeah,' said Col, 'Blyffe is just doin' some gynaecological stuff, some research. I'm helpin'.'

He gesticulated towards a small office where Blyffe, a huge hairy bear of a man with hands the size of Christmas hams filled the room. On the door was written 'Genealogical Research'.

The idea of Blyffe, or Col for that matter, having anything to do with matters gynaecological brought tears to my eyes and I did my best not to laugh. If you tried to make Col up he might sound like a cliché, but he was real and that was the glory of him.

There's always some drama on a TV or film shoot, someone needing a shoulder to cry or lean on. Mostly it's nothing, but to Col, if someone was in strife, he'd amble up and say, as gently as his barking voice could, 'You right? Wanna cuppa? Bickie? Bit of a chat? You right?'

It was always done unobtrusively and struck me as oddly gentle from such a roughneck. More fool me. A gentle, caring soul comes in all sorts of bindings.

Col never got invited, let alone mentioned, at awards, never got a picture in magazines or on news sites, but was always the first to congratulate those who did. I asked him once why it mattered to him.

He said it mattered that people he liked did well. It made him happy. Even a goose like me.

Rough as guts but sweet, generous and caring. Hooroo, Col. Travel well.

•

Sometimes you hear of someone dropping off the perch and you know it's time to gather.

The Uniting Church was the only place on the peninsula that could hold the amount of people who wanted to come to farewell Barry Bolton. Known to many as 'Bazza', he was mayor of the peninsula, President of the RSL, marriage celebrant, schoolteacher and member of so many worthy community groups you'd have thought he wouldn't have had time to have been married for sixty years and have reared three sons with his wife, Shirley.

Whenever I saw him or bumped into him and asked how he was, he'd invariably reply, 'Flat out like a lizard drinking.' When lizards drink, they move their tongues incredibly quickly and flatten and stretch their bodies out, thus the expression.

He always gave this answer, despite the fact that he never really seemed to be in a hurry for anything, or that busy.

His eldest son, Brett, gave the eulogy and mentioned how Barry, in his role as marriage celebrant, had thrown his hat in the ring to administer the vows at the marriage of the Prince of Wales and Lady Diana Spencer.

Despite being an avowed Republican, he thought he might have been able to do a slap-up job either at the Redcliffe Cascades, just behind the War Memorial Swimming Pool and along the banks of Humpybong Creek, or, if that was unavailable, there was a possibility of a particularly lovey garden up in Scarborough. All free of charge, of course.

To his eternal delight, he received a letter from the Queen's private secretary gratefully acknowledging the offer but sadly having to decline Bazza's services as other arrangements had been made.

'That's where they went wrong, you know,' said Barry, 'not using me.'

Probably one of the reasons Barry was an alderman on the council for so long was the number of votes he got from people he'd married.

As legend goes, at a particular marriage ceremony, when the cue was given to play the selected piece of music, when the 'play' button was hit on the tape recorder, instead of the selected song, the hearty tones of Mr Bolton's speech practice boomed forth. Never one to be fazed, he paused, then sagely suggested to the bride and groom, 'Listen to this bit, it's very good. It's about dog licences.'

The odd fact about funerals is that they are in part a reunion and get-together with old faces and acquaintances, so when somebody crashes into the back of me, as I am trying to look suitably formal, with the words, 'Get out of the way, you great idiot,' it only takes a moment or two for me to recognise The Grink, Scott Grinke. Although he is in suit and tie, he is of course behaving much like he did as a sixteen-year-old. And when I recognise him, I follow suit.

Then the legend of Beetle appears. Mark O'Brien, now a successful businessperson, but at one time one of the most creative marker of odds in the Southern Hemisphere. He used to run a book on how long the saying of the Lord's Prayer would take at morning assembly, but to me his work in a Citizenship Education class sealed his legend.

Asked to draw the Redcliffe City coat of arms, instead of trying to copy the city crest, he simply drew a long coat with an endless amount of arms.

I laughed so much we were both given detention.

There is Trevor Bane, Keith 'You're Still a Hottie' Wood, Jill Rushton, Anne Statham, Mr Chappell and the inimitable Jacko, plumber to the stars. Jacko is forced to tell his 'Five Dollar note' story endlessly. This involves the payment to him for some plumbing work done by another teaching colleague of Barry Bolton's, who was occasionally the most infuriating reciter in the Lord's Prayer stakes run by Beetle.

It was hard to tell if he'd forgotten it or was trying to do a Bob Hawke impersonation, so many 'Ahhhs' and pauses were involved.

Jacko was paid a sizeable amount in individual five-dollar notes at the end of the month because the old ex-teacher was trying to win a lucky five-dollar note serial number run by the 4KQ radio station.

'It was like hitting the jackpot because Nanna had forgotten how many five-dollar notes she'd given you in an envelope for your tenth birthday,' deadpanned Jacko.

So many different people from so many different parts of the community where I'd grown up, all coming together to farewell and remember a life.

No life is perfect but there are some so well lived that they reach out and touch so many other fellow citizens.

Sometimes we don't get a chance to say goodbye. Life can be like that. It may not seem fair, but then life doesn't seem to care about fairness. Life goes on until it ends, and for those of us who keep on living we are left to try to make sense of things.

A life I had a little to do with ended not so long ago. Suddenly and without warning. People I have loved have died, but not suddenly. Usually you are already going down a path of grieving, of trying to make sense of an impending loss — and that can be awful and sad beyond any words I could ever write.

But sudden death strikes with an abruptness that shocks and stops you in your tracks. It reminds you of your own mortality, something that we aren't often encouraged to think about, especially on a Saturday morning. And yet perhaps we should think about it occasionally.

Sudden death. A heart attack. My mate had been sitting with his wife and then gone to another room. And had a heart attack. And died. Alone.

We all do that, I suppose. Die, alone.

Yet it strikes me as sad.

He was a good and decent man. He lived a good life. He was a loved husband, father and friend. It's a gift to have known him.

He was one of those people you felt comfortable with. Good company. Someone who was good to sit and spend time with.

A year or two ago, I remember sitting by the water's edge with him on Moreton Island, having a cup of tea and just enjoying each other's company.

I can't remember what we spoke about, but I remember we laughed a lot as we looked out across the bay. When the weekend had come to an end and we said our goodbyes, I remember he shook my hand and, instead of just saying goodbye, he nodded and mumbled, 'I'll see you somewhere down the track.'

It struck me as being quite a sweet and sentimental way of saying goodbye, blokey but quite emotional.

A week or so after I heard of his death, I suddenly remembered him telling me a joke years ago. And I laughed. It was good a joke and he was a good man.

What to do? I remember my dad occasionally coming up to me, seemingly out of the blue, and telling me he loved me. Why? My mother said it was because my old man had lost a lot of friends suddenly during his war years and he wanted to let the people he loved know how much they meant.

I remembered that. And I told my family and friends that I loved them. Maybe they thought it was odd. But, sometimes, we don't get a chance to say goodbye.

But maybe we can be remembered for our part in someone's life and in that remembrance there's a lesson for us.

I was once in a production of Shakespeare's Scottish tragedy, the Macca one. I was a general dogsbody, doing some small parts. When it came time to let Macca know Birnam Wood was moving towards his castle in Dunsinane and all his vaulting ambition had come to nothing, something interesting occurred.

The wood wasn't moving really, the opposition had camouflaged itself in branches, but Macca didn't know that. All he knew was the witches' prophecy about his doom had come to fruition. That's not interesting, just a plot device.

The interesting thing occurred when I wandered out to tell him of this fact, and I had what's referred to as a 'dry'. I forgot some words. Well, one word. The name of the wood. I couldn't find it anywhere in the Teledex upstairs. At first, the bloke playing Macca thought I was pausing for effect but when I finally uttered 'Sherwood Wood had come to Dunsinane', the look he gave me was priceless.

Somehow, I'd combined Shakespeare's great drama with Robin Hood and his merry men. My delivery of this new addition to Shakespeare's great work was rather a stop-start affair and, to make matters worse, I paused after the first syllable of Sherwood before running the next two words together. So, it sounded like I was telling Macca someone called Sher Woodwood was coming around for a cup of tea.

Macca said ruefully, 'Sher Woodwood, eh? A bad day indeed.'

As Shakespeare rolled in his grave, I felt a complete flog, but the fellow playing Macca came up to me after the performance, gave a smile, slapped me on the shoulder and asked if Sher was the actor Edward Woodwood's sister.

How he finished the play I'll never know. Everybody had a fit of the giggles after my line, it was lucky Macca had already uttered the words which are some of the most beautifully terrifying ever written in the English language:

> Life's but a walking shadow, a poor player
> That struts and frets his hour upon the stage,
> And then is heard no more. It is a tale
> Told by an idiot, full of sound and fury,
> Signifying nothing.

Whatever we think we are, whatever we've achieved, we're temporal. Finite. Tough stuff when you think about it. But because we're human beings, we can look at things the way only a human can.

The actor who played Macca died some years ago. I wonder if the utter bleak despair of Shakespeare's words were with him as he contemplated his own death. Perhaps. But as he lay in a hospital bed surrounded by his family, he, of all things, laughed. His wife asked why.

He said he was thinking of 'Bloody McInnes' and his Sherwood Wood. 'Stupid bugger could have at least come up with another wood, but, no, he went with a forest.' And he laughed again.

What a great bloke. The family sent a card to me, by way of thanks for being a part of his life, but really, I thank him. Living and laughing right till the end. Not a bad message to go out on.

•

The things we think about as we go about our everyday lives can come to define us. That was the interesting thing with the Covid pandemic: we hadn't been confronted with something that was a threat to us all for quite a time. But now that thought was always there, even when cooking an omelette.

The overriding suspicion I hold, even before I begin cooking an omelette, is I know how it will end – as a variant of scrambled eggs. A quite tasty mess of bits and pieces that I will wolf down like a hungry kelpie but not the fluffy omelette of my imagination or even anything resembling the illustration on my digital tablet of the ultimate 'Foolproof Omelette'.

Well, this recipe is about to meet its match. I am, if nothing else, a Fool's fool.

I listen to the news as I cook, for my sins.

Various politicians and other shouty pontificating talking heads begin to blame each other for the cost of living crisis, inflation, the housing crisis and even Covid.

I wonder if I've put in too much milk.

Covid was a dangerous and unpleasant virus which has created dangerous and unpleasant environments and moods.

I add some pepper and salt, and maybe some oregano, and I wish we would all cut each other some slack.

Not every decision we make will be right; in fact, some probably will be wrong, but hopefully they will be less wrong each time.

My foolproof recipe seems to be imploding as I consult the recipe and then decide I'll add another egg.

There's news about two black holes colliding somewhere in some suburb in space. This alarms me for a moment because it sounds like something out of a bad disaster movie.

I listen, as I shuffle the foolproof omelette, to an astrophysicist talking about the black holes the same way I talk about the idea of a XXXX Draught beer at the Breakfast Creek Hotel – a little too enthusiastically.

He's lost me after a while. I remember a maths teacher calling me a black hole because I was so dense nothing could penetrate me.

But don't they collapse? Or suck in things? I turn my attention away, like a fool, from my foolproof omelette. I get out my phone and google, 'What happens when something gets sucked into a black hole?'

I read about matter being torn apart and squeezed.

'Jesus Christ,' I mutter and toss the phone on the kitchen bench.

The astrophysicist is asked what the black holes mean for us on earth.

There's a moment's pause and, despite myself, I stop what I'm doing and listen. I want to know.

'Well, in the scheme of things,' the astrophysicist eventually says, 'not much. We're good to go.'

I laugh. I like that phrase, it's peculiarly Australian.

Nothing inspires action, confidence and good feelings as much as Australia's 'good to go'. It's full of positivity.

Despite all that's put in our way, the obstacles people and things create – black holes, bad manners, pandemics, politicians – most of us, at any and perhaps all times, are 'Good to go'.

This phrase is perfect for this time.

It says that we are not only unbeaten but are there for others. What we have we share; whether good, bad or indifferent.

And speaking of indifferent, I look at my foolproof omelette.

Yeah, nah. It has morphed yet again into scrambled eggs.

Never mind, I am good to go!

ACKNOWLEDGEMENTS

I would like to acknowledge, in no particular order of importance, the following: Karen Ward, Deonie Fiford, Fiona Hazard, all at Hachette, Bernadette Foley, The Fly!, Sahara, Pizza Feet, Bevan Bleakley, Rick McCosker, Paleface Adios, Peter Bolton, Captain Jeremy, Foxy Danbar, Hang On Snoopy, Vaughan, Laurie, Rhian, Corby, Niall Mather, The Flying Carona, Spirios Arion, Clem McInnes, Gene McInnes, Fi and Merge, The Little Chickens, The Wee Murderer, Amanda Higgs and Ray.

William McInnes is one of Australia's most popular writers and actors. His books include the bestselling memoirs *A Man's Got to Have a Hobby* and *That'd Be Right*. In 2012 his book *Worse Things Happen at Sea*, co-written with his wife, Sarah Watt, was named the best non-fiction title in the ABIA and Indie Book Awards.

Also an award-winning actor and best known for his leading roles in *Blue Heelers*, *SeaChange*, *Total Control* and *The Newsreader*, William has won two Logies and two AFI/AACTA Awards for Best Actor in the film *Unfinished Sky* and Best Supporting Actor in *The Newsreader*.

William grew up in Queensland and lives in Melbourne.